DATE DUE

ROBOT WORLD

ROBOTS IN SPACE

by Jenny Fretland VanVoorst

pogo

Ideas for Parents and Teachers

Pogo Books let children practice reading informational text while introducing them to nonfiction features such as headings, labels, sidebars, maps, and diagrams, as well as a table of contents, glossary, and index.

Carefully leveled text with a strong photo match offers early fluent readers the support they need to succeed.

Before Reading

- "Walk" through the book and point out the various nonfiction features. Ask the student what purpose each feature serves.
- Look at the glossary together. Read and discuss the words.

Read the Book

- Have the child read the book independently.
- Invite him or her to list questions that arise from reading.

After Reading

- Discuss the child's questions. Talk about how he or she might find answers to those questions.
- Prompt the child to think more. Ask: Can you think of another environment where robots could go more safely than people? What other dangerous jobs do you think robots could be used for?

Pogo Books are published by Jump!
5357 Penn Avenue South
Minneapolis, MN 55419
www.jumplibrary.com

Library of Congress Cataloging-in-Publication Data

Fretland VanVoorst, Jenny, 1972-
  Robots in space / by Jenny Fretland VanVoorst.
    pages cm. – (Robot world)
  Includes bibliographical references and index.
  ISBN 978-1-62031-219-3 (hardcover: alk. paper) –
  ISBN 978-1-62496-306-3 (ebook)
  1. Robots–Juvenile literature.
  2. Space robotics–Juvenile literature. I. Title.
  TL1097.F745 2015
  629.43–dc23

                                2015020999

Series Designer: Anna Peterson
Photo Researchers: Anna Peterson and Michelle Sonnek

Photo Credits: Alamy, 18-19; Corbis, 1, 14-15, 16; NASA, 6-7, 10-11, 12-13, 17, 20-21, 23; Science Source, cover, 3; Shutterstock, 4, 5, 8, 9.

Printed in the United States of America at Corporate Graphics in North Mankato, Minnesota.

To Liam—JFV

TABLE OF CONTENTS

CHAPTER 1

WHAT DO THEY DO?

Have you ever wanted to visit Mars? Explore the moon? It sounds exciting. But it is also very dangerous. There's no air for us to breathe. Food and water are nowhere to be found.

But robots don't need air. They don't need food or water. They just need a source of power and a set of instructions.

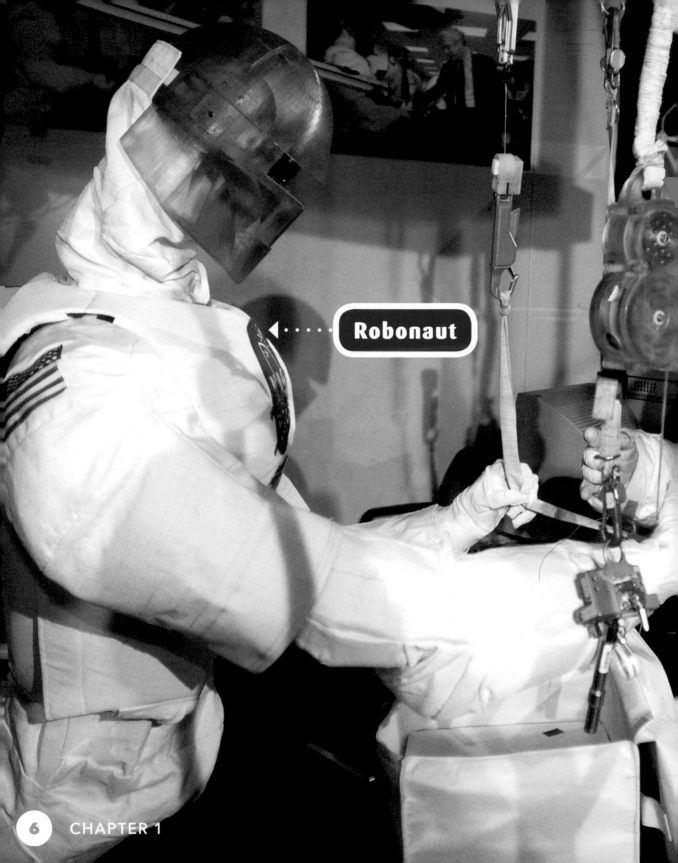

Robonaut

Space robots orbit Earth. They work inside the **International Space Station**. They explore other planets. Some space robots serve as human helpers. Others do things that people can't—at least not right now.

DID YOU KNOW?

Robots work off of **programs**. A program is a set of directions. It tells a robot what to do in great detail. It leaves no room for error.

1 ....
2 ....
3 ....
4 ....
5 ....

CHAPTER 2

HOW DO THEY WORK?

Robots that work as human helpers are often remote controlled.

Other robots work independently. Robots on a distant planet can't depend on people for directions. They are too far away.

As a result, many space robots are **autonomous**. They gather **data** about their surroundings. Then they use that data to decide how to act.

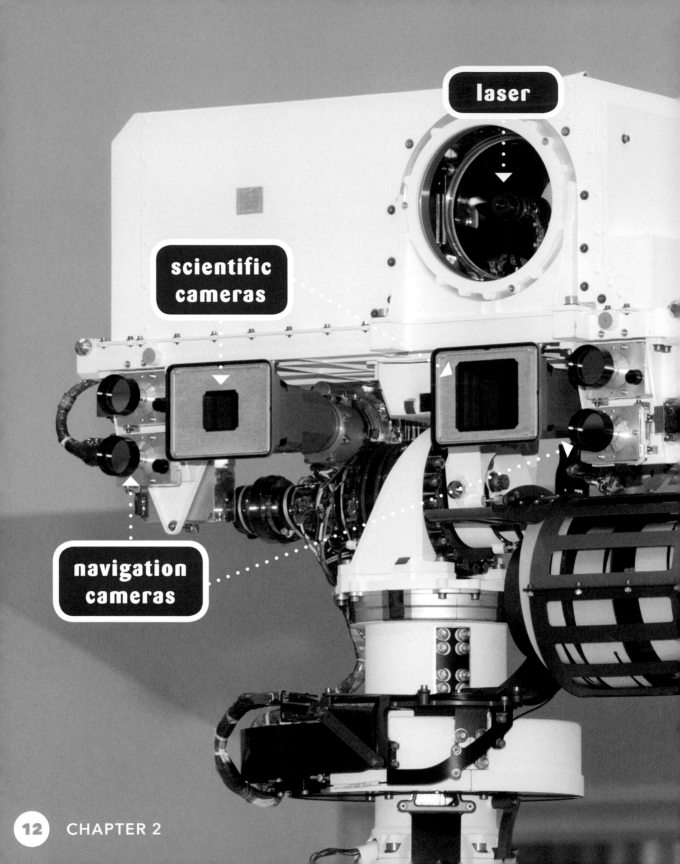

laser

scientific
cameras

navigation
cameras

Space robots gather data using **sensors**. They might have cameras and **GPS**. They might have **lidar** or **radar**. They may have a hand that senses pressure.

If a rock is in a robot's path, the robot will use its sensors to spot what else is around it. Then its computer uses that information to find a safe path.

TAKE A LOOK!

Robots sense what's around them. They "think" about the next step. Then they take action. This is called the sense-think-act cycle. Not all robots are capable of all three steps. But many space robots are.

1. SENSE

2. THINK

3. ACT

CHAPTER 3

MEET THE ROBOTS

We build robots to do jobs that a person would otherwise do. That's why many robots are based on the human form. For example, Robonaut looks like a human **torso**.

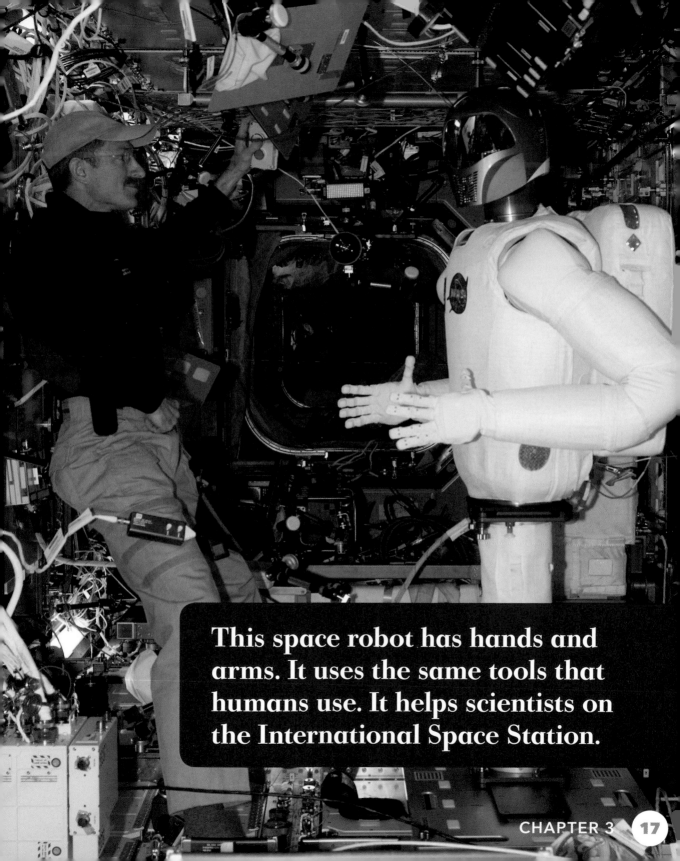

This space robot has hands and arms. It uses the same tools that humans use. It helps scientists on the International Space Station.

Curiosity is a Mars **rover**. It is an autonomous robot. It has a program. But it senses, thinks, and acts to carry it out.

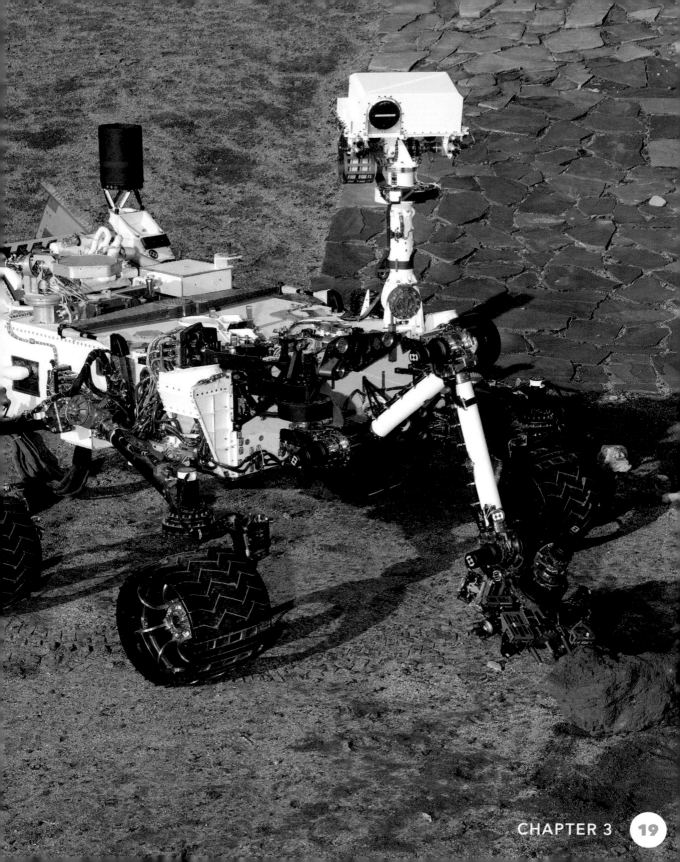

drill
holes

Curiosity collects data. It does experiments. Because of it, we know things about Mars we otherwise never could.

Where do you think robots will go next? What do you think they will teach us?

ACTIVITIES & TOOLS

ROBOT SENSING

Senses are very important for robots. Try this experiment to learn what it takes to get a robot to "think" and act.

- blindfold
- items to create an obstacle course (chairs, pillows, cushions, boxes)

❶ Set up an obstacle course in a safe place in your home or yard. Create simple, narrow paths with some twists and turns.

❷ Blindfold a friend and bring her to the obstacle course. Explain to her that she's a remote-controlled robot and that you are the controller. For her to get through the course, she has to use her sense of hearing to listen to your instructions. She also needs to use her sense of touch to be aware of obstacles in her path.

❸ Give very specific instructions for your robot to follow – literally step by step.

❹ After your friend finishes the course, talk about what instructions were helpful and which were not. Then let your friend recreate the obstacle course and have you follow her commands. Compare experiences as both robot and controller.

GLOSSARY

autonomous: Able to make certain decisions without human input.

data: Facts about something that can be used in calculating, reasoning, or planning.

GPS: A navigation system that uses satellite signals to find the location of a radio receiver on or above the earth's surface; abbreviation of global positioning system.

International Space Station: A structure orbiting Earth where scientists live and work, performing experiments in space.

lidar: A device that uses laser beams to detect and locate objects.

program: A set of instructions that a robot follows.

radar: A device that uses radio waves to detect and locate objects.

rover: A kind of mobile exploratory robot designed to move over rough ground.

sensors: Onboard tools that serve as a robot's eyes, ears, and other sense organs so that the robot can create a picture of the environment in which it operates.

torso: A person's upper body, from the waist up.

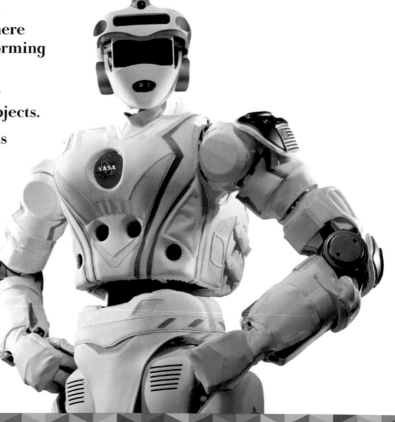

INDEX

TO LEARN MORE

Learning more is as easy as 1, 2, 3.

1) Go to www.factsurfer.com

2) Enter "robotsinspace" into the search box.

3) Click the "Surf" to see a list of websites.

With factsurfer, finding more information is just a click away.

My debt to history is one which
cannot be calculated. I know of no other
motivation which so accounts for my
awakening interest as a young lad in the
principles of leadership and government. . . .
I know that the one great external influence
which, more than anything else,
nourished and sustained that interest in
government and public service was the endless
reading of history which I began as a boy
and which I have kept up ever since.

HARRY TRUMAN

The unparalleled rise of America
has not been the result of riches in lands,
forests, or mines; it sprang from
the ideas and ideals which liberated minds
and stimulated the spirits of men.
In those ideas and ideals are the soul
of the people. No American can
review this vast pageant of progress without
confidence and faith, without courage, strength,
and resolution for the future.

HERBERT HOOVER

Kennedy: "A Nation of Immigrants," New York, 1959
Eisenhower: Reader's Digest, October, 1948
Truman: "Memoirs," © 1955, Time Inc.
Hoover: 150th anniversary address, Yorktown, Va., October 19, 1931

Important Dates and Events to Remember
1774-1783

1774 June 1, British close port of Boston. September 5, First Continental Congress meets in Philadelphia. Delegates from all colonies except Georgia attend.

1775 April 18, to impede activities of patriots, General Gage sends British troops to Lexington and Concord to seize rebel leaders and supplies.
Patriot Paul Revere rides to warn Americans of the British movement.
April 19, American Revolution begins at Lexington Green, where patriots and redcoats trade musket shots. Eight Americans are killed, 10 wounded. At Concord, Americans turn back the British at North Bridge.
May 10, Ethan Allen and Green Mountain Boys capture Fort Ticonderoga.
Second Continental Congress meets.
June 15, Congress appoints George Washington commander in chief of the Continental army.
June 17, Battle of Bunker Hill (fought on Breed's Hill), Massachusetts. Well-entrenched rebels deal heavy losses to redcoats, but finally must retreat.
December 31, Battle of Quebec. Defeat of forces of Benedict Arnold and Richard Montgomery on Plains of Abraham end American hopes in Canada.

1776 January 10, *Common Sense*, Thomas Paine's argument for independence, is published in Philadelphia.
March 4, Americans under Washington entrench on Dorchester Heights, forcing General William Howe's troops to evacuate Boston (March 17).
April 13, Washington's army marches to New York City, fortifies the area.

July 4, Congress accepts Declaration of Independence, drafted by Jefferson.
July 12, British fleet under Admiral Richard Howe anchors in New York Bay.
August 27-29, Battle of Long Island, New York. Washington's troops, caught between enemy army and navy, narrowly escape complete destruction by retreating to New York. Americans fight Hessian mercenaries for the first time.
September 15, British occupy New York.
September 22, Nathan Hale is captured and hanged as a spy by the British.
October 28, Battle of White Plains, New York. Feverish contest with Howe's army ends in American retreat (November 10).
November 16, Americans surrender Fort Washington, New York, to the British.
November 20, redcoats take Fort Lee, New Jersey, forcing Washington, on November 21, to race the British across the state to save Philadelphia.
December 19, Thomas Paine's *American Crisis* rallies patriots' spirits.
December 26, Battle of Trenton, New Jersey. Washington surprises Hessians on morning after Christmas, wins easily.

1777 January 3, Battle of Princeton, New Jersey: 8,000 redcoats escaping capture at Trenton are trapped and defeated.
July 6, British under Burgoyne capture Fort Ticonderoga and 128 cannon.
July 23, Howe sails troops to Chesapeake Bay to spring surprise attack on Philadelphia from the South.
August 16, Battle of Bennington, Vermont. Hessians sent by Burgoyne for supplies are caught in patriots' crossfire. Burgoyne is forced to retreat to Saratoga, New York.

September 11, Battle of Brandywine, Pennsylvania, claims 12,000 patriots as Washington fails to stop Howe's march.
September 19, first Battle of Saratoga. Burgoyne tries unsuccessfully to break out of an American trap.
September 26, British take Philadelphia.
October 3-4, Battle of Germantown, Pennsylvania. Washington makes costly error in plan to chase British from area.
October 7, second Battle of Saratoga. Again, Burgoyne cannot break through the American line.
October 17, Burgoyne surrenders. The victory stirs France to aid the American cause (treaty of February 6, 1778).
December 17, Americans camp at Valley Forge, Pennsylvania. Winter is severe and supplies short; 2,500 men die.

1778   June 18, Clinton, fearing attack by combined French and American forces, leaves Philadelphia for New York City, believing it easier to defend.
June 28, Battle of Monmouth, New Jersey. American ambush of Clinton's army ends in a bloody stalemate.
July 11, French fleet under Admiral d'Estaing arrives in America.
December 29, British troops drive Continentals from Savannah, Georgia.

1779   February 25, George Rogers Clark's rangers capture Vincennes.
July 16, Anthony Wayne's troops secure British works at Stony Point, New York.
September 16, Siege of Savannah. Combined assault by French navy under d'Estaing and Benjamin Lincoln's patriots begins, but is abandoned in October.
September 23, off English coast, John Paul Jones on *Bon Homme Richard* overcomes the British warship *Serapis*.

1780   May 12, Siege of Charleston, South Carolina, by British brings greatest American loss of war.

July 10, Count Jean de Rochambeau lands at Newport with French soldiers.
August 16, Battle of Camden, South Carolina. Horatio Gates' defeat endangers Continental army in the South.
September 23, capture of John André reveals Benedict Arnold's plot to betray West Point. André is tried and hanged. Arnold escapes (October 2).
October 7, Battle of Kings Mountain, North Carolina. Redcoats under Patrick Ferguson, rallying loyalist recruits, take a drubbing from Continentals.

1781   January 17, Battle of Hannah's Cowpens, South Carolina, is disastrous loss for British.
January through February, Nathanael Greene's retreat through South lures Cornwallis 200 miles from his supplies.
March 15, Battle of Guilford Court House, North Carolina. Cornwallis catches up with Greene, destroys one quarter of his force, captures his guns.
August 1, to protect his army, Cornwallis moves to a more defensible position at Yorktown, Virginia.
August 19, pretending attack on New York, Washington marches army in three columns southward through New Jersey.
August 30, Admiral de Grasse, commanding a French fleet, anchors in Lynnhaven Bay, near Yorktown.
September 28, Siege of Yorktown. Allied armies, led by Washington, Rochambeau, and Lafayette, reach city. They begin bombardment on October 9.
October 14, Redoubts 9 and 10—keys to British defenses at Yorktown—fall.
October 19, Washington accepts formal surrender of Cornwallis' army.

1783   April 19, Continental army receives official announcement of "cessation of hostilities" with Great Britain.
November 25, British leave New York. Washington bids his officers farewell.

We hold these truths to be self-evident, that all men are created equal, that they are endowed by their Creator with certain unalienable Rights, that among these are Life, Liberty and the pursuit of Happiness. That to secure these rights, Governments are instituted among Men, deriving their just powers from the consent of the governed. That whenever any Form of Government becomes destructive of these ends, it is the Right of the People to alter or to abolish it, and to institute new Government, laying its foundation on such principles and organizing its powers in such form, as to them shall seem most likely to effect their Safety and Happiness.

THE GOLDEN BOOK

HISTORY
of the
UNITED STATES

by **EARL SCHENCK MIERS**
LITT. B., M. A., L. H. D.

Paintings by **ALTON S. TOBEY**

Drawings by **RICHARD P. KLUGA**

Technical Consultants:
L. ETHAN ELLIS AND RICHARD M. BROWN
of the Department of History, Rutgers University

HERBERT J. SANBORN, *Art Research*

**VOLUME
3**

**THE AGE OF
REVOLUTION**

GOLDEN PRESS **NEW YORK**

How To Use This Volume THE AGE OF REVOLUTION tells the story of the American Revolution, ending with victory at Yorktown, and may be read from cover to cover. It discusses many events that took place over a long span of time. The events taken up in each chapter are described briefly at the opening of the chapter and also on the contents page. This will allow the reader to find any subject he wants quickly and easily. Each section of the text also has the dates of the period it covers printed in blue at the top of the page. The principal events and the dates on which they occurred are listed in the timetable on the inside front cover. Maps are included throughout the text, and also on the inside back cover. An index for the entire series is contained in Volume X.

CONTENTS ~ THE AGE OF REVOLUTION

Library of Congress Catalog Card Number: 63-9433

© copyright 1963 by Golden Press, Inc. and The Ridge Press, Inc. Printed in the U.S.A. by Western Printing and Lithographing Co.

Designed and produced by
The Ridge Press, Inc.
17 East 45th Street, New York, N. Y.

Roost of Rebels

British soldiers close the port of Boston, but the citizens of the city show that they are not ready to give up without a struggle.

Bostonians scowled as British redcoats—"bloody-backs"—under General Thomas Gage paraded through the streets. In the harbor British men-of-war rode at anchor, their guns turned on the wharves and homes of old Boston.

It was June 1, 1774, and everyone was waiting for the church bells to sound the hour of noon. Then, officially, the port of Boston would be closed to all trade and travel. By punishing this one city George III intended to teach the rest of the American colonies a lesson. They could expect the same treatment if they followed Boston's example and defied the royal government.

The "bloody-backs" had orders to shoot anyone who made the least resistance to the blockade. Even so, General Gage was uneasy. Although the king believed that Gage's four regiments could handle anything that developed, the king did not know much about America. Boston alone had 15,000 inhabitants, and Massachusetts about 400,000. If the New Englanders decided to fight, they could quickly overcome Gage's puny force.

Gage had been in America nine years and had married the daughter of a prominent family in New Jersey. He was governor of Massachusetts as well as general of the army. He knew these people. He had fought with George Washington when Braddock had failed at Fort DuQuesne, and he knew how Americans could fight. They were tough, hardy, and strong-minded.

Gage did his job well. Boston became a city of living ghosts. No merchant vessels could enter its harbor. Not one pound of hay, not one sheep or calf, could be landed at any wharf. Not a single passenger could be ferried across the river to Charlestown. Soldiers stood everywhere, and cannon pointed down from every hill, ready to fire at the first sign of an uprising. British warships stood guard in the harbor.

THE COLONIES AID BOSTON

But the Bostonians soon found that they did not stand alone. Aid poured in from everywhere in the colonies. "Don't pay for a single ounce of tea," said Christopher Gadsden of South Carolina, who sent 200 barrels of rice and promised to send 800 more. Old Israel Putnam, a veteran of the French and Indian War, walked almost a hundred miles from his farm in Connecticut to lead a flock of one hundred sheep to Boston. From Georgia came sixty barrels of rice, from French Quebec 1,000 bushels of wheat, from Wilmington, North Carolina, 2,000 pounds in cash that had been raised

within a week. Marblehead and Salem, old rivals in trade, opened their wharves to Boston merchants. From little New England villages came rye, flour, peas, cattle, oil, and fish. In Virginia, George Washington pledged fifty pounds to help the people of Boston.

THE MINUTEMEN TURN OUT

Once Lord North, the king's chief advisor, had called any union of the American colonies a "rope of sand." Now the colonists replied: "It is a rope of sand that will hang him." In every village, men were drilling with guns. Even small boys drilled with broomsticks for the defense of their homes. Forges glowed and hammers beat upon anvils as blacksmiths made guns, swords, and bayonets. On every farm men were making their own gunpowder and lead bullets. Massachusetts had called 12,000 volunteers to arms. They were known as Minutemen, because they stood ready to fight at a minute's notice.

Gage's worries increased. He ordered new fortifications built, but no Boston carpenter would work for him. To be on the safe side, Gage sent his soldiers to seize the gunpowder that the colonists had stored at Cambridge and Charlestown. Rumors spread as far as the Connecticut River that war had started.

Suddenly the roads swarmed with Minutemen marching on Boston. Some came on foot, with muskets slung across their shoulders. Some came on horses or mules, with swords hanging from their saddlebags. Finally convinced the stories were false, they returned home. It was estimated that 50,000 men had turned out. The "rope of sand" was growing sturdier.

While blacksmiths worked tirelessly making guns, boys drilled with broom handles, and the colonists prepared for the coming war.

THE FIRST CONTINENTAL CONGRESS

Delegates from every colony except Georgia meet in Philadelphia to draw up a list of British wrongs.

In September, 1774, delegates arrived in Philadelphia from every colony except Georgia to organize the First Continental Congress. An argument over voting was settled by giving every colony an equal voice in the debates. The delegates were of various religious beliefs, and a dispute arose over whether each morning session should open with a prayer.

Massachusetts' Sam Adams, a Congregationalist, settled that issue: "I am no bigot. I can hear a prayer from a man of piety and virtue, who, at the same time, is a friend to his country." An Episcopalian minister was selected to give the prayer.

Each morning when the delegates met in Carpenters' Hall, the doors were locked so that their sessions could be kept secret. The delegates might have saved themselves the trouble; Joseph Galloway, leader of the Pennsylvania delegation, was probably a British spy. Otherwise, in the opinion of John Adams, the delegates were "a collection of the greatest men upon this continent in point of abilities, virtues, and fortunes." One thing was certain—they had minds of their own. Some argued that all government in America had ended, others that the situation could still be saved. Excitable Christopher Gadsden called for an immediate declaration of war.

"Our towns are built of wood and brick," he cried. "If they are burned down we can rebuild them, but liberty once lost is gone forever."

On October 8 the delegates resolved:

"That this Congress approve the opposition of the inhabitants of Massachusetts Bay to the execution of the late acts of Parliament; and if the same shall be attempted to be carried into execution by force, in such cases all America ought to support them in their opposition."

THE DECLARATION OF RIGHTS

The delegates drew up a Declaration of Rights, and listed the wrongs that had been done to the colonies by the royal government. They also agreed that the colonies would not use or import British goods, and would not export goods to Britain. This would go on until the government changed

When Sam Adams of Massachusetts spoke, he held his listeners spellbound, whether they were a crowd of Bostonians or the delegates to the First Continental Congress.

its treatment of the colonies. After eight weeks, the delegates decided their work was finished. Sam Adams spoke so that everyone could hear:

"I would advise persisting in our struggle for liberty, though it were revealed from Heaven that 999 men were to perish, and only one of a thousand to survive and retain his liberty. One such freeman must possess more virtue, and enjoy more happiness, than a thousand slaves."

BENJAMIN FRANKLIN IN LONDON

Ben Franklin represents the colonists in England and tells his hosts a fable.

It was soon clear that Americans meant to stand up for their rights, even at the risk of war. In April, another "tea party" took place, this time in New York. When a shipper tried to land a cargo of tea secretly, the Sons of Liberty found out about it and, as in Boston, disguised themselves as Mohawks and dumped it in the harbor. That October, in Annapolis, Maryland, the schooner *Peggy Stewart* was burned because her cargo included seventeen packages of tea. In December, another shipment of tea, this one stored in a warehouse in Greenwich, New Jersey, was set on fire and destroyed.

But the colonists had more on their minds than just destroying British tea. Mills began going up for the manufacture of gunpowder, and Minutemen went out to plow their fields with muskets slung across their backs. Whatever was coming, the colonists were determined to be ready for it.

GAGE SOUNDS THE ALARM

From Boston Gage sent London an alarming report. All New England was preparing for war, he wrote. He did not see how he could be expected to stand off this angry mob with the force he had. Let the mother country cut loose from the colonies. Then the colonies would turn on one another until they were exhausted by their own squabbling. George III answered: "The New England governments are now in a state of rebellion. Blows must decide whether they are to be subject to this country, or are to be independent."

Benjamin Franklin still represented the colonies in London. In a ticklish situation, he wrote a paper entitled, "Hints for Conversation upon the subject of Terms that may probably produce a Durable Union between Britain and the Colonies." Franklin's paper simply suggested that Englishmen in America should enjoy the same rights and privileges as Englishmen in the mother country.

Franklin puzzled the British. He was one of the greatest men of his age—gifted, well educated, quick-witted. He went everywhere in London and knew everyone, and although he made a few enemies, he also made hosts of friends. But the British never really understood Franklin's love of liberty. They were not able to understand how such a man could be so interested in the rights of a few backwoods farmers in America. And although Franklin was a persuasive speaker, he was never able to explain it to them.

By Christmas news of the acts of the Continental Congress reached London, and Franklin's position grew more uncomfortable. When Parliament met in January, 1775, Franklin heard himself described by the Earl of Sandwich as "one of the bitterest and most mischievous enemies this country has ever known." This did not trouble Franklin, who was a skillful diplomat. But as spring came on, he realized that he was wasting his time in London. Entertained by friends one night before he left for America, Franklin made up a fable for them:

THE EAGLE AND THE HARE

"Once upon a time, an eagle soaring around a farmer's barn and espying a hare, darted down upon him like a sunbeam, seized him in his claws, and remounted with him in the air. He soon found that he had a creature of more courage and strength than a hare, for which, not withstanding the keenness of his eyesight, he had mistaken a cat. The snarling and scrambling of the prey was very inconvenient, and, what was worse, she had disengaged herself from his talons, grasped his body with her fore limbs, so as to stop his breath, and seized fast hold of his throat with her teeth.

" 'Pray,' said the eagle, 'let go your hold and I will release you.'

" 'Very fine,' said the cat. 'I have no fancy to fall from this height, and be crushed to death. You have taken me up, and you shall stoop and let me down.' The eagle thought it necessary to stoop accordingly."

Franklin's listeners had only to put England in the place of the eagle and America in the place of the cat to understand the moral.

Franklin charmed the British with his wit and intelligence, but even he was unable to make them understand the colonists' views.

195

*Even the children of Boston were filled with re-
bellion, as Gage found out when a group of boys
complained that British soldiers were inter-
fering with their sledding on Boston Common.*

THE WAR BEGINS

*Paul Revere warns the Minutemen
that the British are advancing on
Concord, and the first shot is
fired in Lexington.*

In February of 1775, some small boys in
Boston were angry. Gage's soldiers kept
knocking down the snow hills they had
built on Boston Common for sledding. The
boys complained to the captain, who would
do nothing. So they carried their complaint
to General Gage, telling him that they had
come "to demand satisfaction." Gage ac-
cused the youngsters of having been taught
"rebellion" by their fathers.

The boys stood their ground. Coming to
Gage had been their own idea. For the third
time yesterday their snow hills had been
trampled down by the soldiers, and the captain had laughed at their complaint. "We
will bear it no longer," they said.

Gage shook his head. "The very children
here," he told a fellow officer, "draw in a
love of liberty with the air they breathe."
Then, turning to the boys, he added: "Be
assured that if any troops trouble you again,
they shall be punished."

Gage could be mild with the boys, but he
would have to deal more harshly with their
fathers. There was no doubt that the colonists were ready to revolt. Patrick Henry
put into words what they all felt when he
spoke at St. John's Church in Richmond,
Virginia, that spring. He said, "Is life so
dear or peace so sweet as to be purchased at
the price of chains and slavery? Forbid it,
Almighty God! I know not what course
others may take, but as for me, give me liberty or give me death!"

By April, Gage had decided to act. He
would bag Sam Adams and John Hancock,
and ship them to England to stand trial for
treason. Then he would march to Concord
and seize the materials for war that the patriots were storing there—muskets, cannon,
gunpowder in barrels, spades, axes, medi-
cine chests, tents, flour, beef, salt. To do this
job, Gage chose his strongest troops, the
grenadiers, and his fastest, the light infantry. He would act on the night of April 18,
and he tried to keep the date a secret.

But men like Paul Revere, the silver-
smith, and Joseph Warren, a doctor, had
organized a vigilance committee to watch
for just such things. On April 15 they saw

the British hauling up their rowboats for repairs. They knew that Gage was preparing to move some of his troops. But how—by land or by water? They had to know, so that they could warn Adams and Hancock, who were staying with a friend in Lexington before leaving for the Second Continental Congress in Philadelphia. And so they arranged with the sexton of Old North Church to give the signal when the time came—two lanterns in the belfry if the British left Boston by water, one lantern if they marched over Boston Neck by land.

Following a day of showers, the night of April 18 was clear and cold. At about ten o'clock 800 British troops marched to their boats from Boston Common and two lanterns flashed in the belfry of Old North Church. Paul Revere leaped onto a horse he had borrowed from Deacon Larkin and rode through the streets of slumbering Charlestown.

The smell of salt marshes rose to greet him as he fled along the road with the Mystic River on his right and the Charles on his left. Two British sentinels challenged him, but Revere spun his horse about, raked the animal's flanks with his spurs, and escaped at a gallop. Soon he was rattling over the bridge into Medford, shouting that the British were coming. He went on, crying the same message at almost every farmhouse,

197

until a little past midnight when he rode into Lexington to warn Adams and Hancock. Revere rode on toward Concord, only to be captured by the British.

THE BATTLE OF LEXINGTON

But already bells were ringing in Lexington. Minutemen were jumping from their beds, snatching up their muskets, and rushing to the Lexington Green. Here Captain John Parker called the roll and ordered them to charge their guns with powder and ball. The men waited in the chilly night air, pounding the ground with their feet to keep warm. Some began to believe the alarm was false and drifted home to bed. Others decided to spend the night in Buckman's Tavern.

Then the alarm bells rang again, and this time there was no mistake. The British redcoats under Major John Pitcairn were less than two miles from Lexington. The Minutemen came back on the run, lining up beside tall Captain Parker.

In the gray light of early morning, April 19, 1775, Major Pitcairn galloped into town at the head of his "bloody-backs." He paused at the sight of the Minutemen, then called out an order:

"Disperse, you villains! Lay down your arms!"

He repeated the order several times, and the Minutemen slowly began to move away, still carrying their guns. Then, suddenly, a shot rang out. Nobody knew who fired it, but it set off a volley from the redcoats. The war had come, with young Jonathan Harrington beating his drum and every man taking care of himself.

The scene on Lexington Green quickly became one of mad disorder. Harrington died there, silent with his drum. A British ball buckled the knees of Jonas Parker, the captain's cousin. John Brown fell at the edge of the swamp, just north of the Green.

The redcoats seemed to go out of hand, firing even after Pitcairn called to them to stop. The Battle of Lexington lasted only minutes. Eight Massachusetts men died, ten were wounded. A slight leg wound to one redcoat was the only British casualty.

Sam Adams, lingering in his flight to freedom, heard the sounds of battle and shouted at the wind: "What a glorious morning for America is this!" Adams and Hancock were well on their way to safety by the time Pitcairn had lined up his victorious troops on the Green. The major waited while his men gave three cheers, then, tight-lipped, led them down the road toward Concord.

Through the slumbering countryside, Paul Revere rode on his way to Lexington and Concord, warning the colonial militiamen that the British were coming.

The Battle of Lexington Green was a short one. The well-disciplined British regulars soon were able to drive off the colonists, but the skirmish delayed the British march and allowed more Minutemen to assemble at Concord.

Victory

AT THE BRIDGE

*Minutemen swarm into Concord and
defeat the British, who are forced
to retreat back to Boston.*

The people of Concord awakened at
about two o'clock in the morning to the
ringing of the alarm bell. Minutemen tum-
bled out of bed and ran to the Green. Some
leaped onto horses and rode to neighboring
towns to spread the warning.

There was work for everyone that night.
Boys and girls helped to carry supplies into
the woods where they would be secure from
the redcoats. Walking on each side of the
oxen, the youngsters whipped the animals
into a trot until the carts were bouncing
down the road. Meanwhile, the Committee
of Safety—a group of citizens responsible for
the defense of the town—huddled together,
discussing where to make their stand.

Early morning brought the sounds of
fighting at Lexington. Colonel James Barrett, who had proved his qualities as a
fighter in the French and Indian War, stationed his Concord forces on a hill near the
village.

Men were now coming from surrounding
communities—from Lincoln and Acton,
Carlisle and Chelmsford, Weston and Lit-
tleton. Barrett decided that his position on
the hill left him too exposed and moved his
force to rising ground beyond North
Bridge, a mile or so from Concord Green.
Sooner than anyone expected, the British
arrived, stepping smartly in two columns,
one coming by the main road and the other
over the hill that the Americans had just
vacated.

Swarming over Concord in search of supplies, the redcoats soon saw how well the
citizens had done their work in the hours
before dawn. They found some barrels of

flour, wooden plates, spoons—and that was
about all. They cut down and burned a
Liberty Pole and set the courthouse on fire.

Other redcoats rushed to destroy North
Bridge. Here the Minutemen surged forward, to be hit by a volley from the "bloody-
backs."

"Fire, fellow soldiers," said a Massachusetts major. "For God's sake, fire!"

The Minutemen raised their muskets to
their shoulders. They fired, and three British regulars fell dead.

The fire of the Minutemen went on.
Dazed and confused, the redcoats fell back,
leaving North Bridge in possession of the
Americans. The British officers could hardly
believe what was happening. The king's
best troops were retreating from farmers.

Nor was it an easy retreat. The countryside was alive with Minutemen, and one

In the early dawn the men of Concord awaited the British, while their wives and children moved the colonists' supplies to the safety of the woods.

British officer wrote afterward, "The Americans seemed to drop from the clouds." They were behind every tree, every wall, every barn, every twist and dip in the road. The weary redcoats staggered back into Lexington, saved from surrender by the arrival of reinforcements. By nightfall they limped into Boston.

Every colony in America was stirred by the success at Concord. New Hampshire voted to raise an army of 2,000 to help Massachusetts, Connecticut set its quota at 6,000, Rhode Island at 1,500.

Within Boston, Gage agreed to give safe conduct out of the city to all who surrendered their weapons. But the people who were loyal to the crown—the Sons of Liberty called them Tories—raised an outcry. They wanted Gage to hold those with patriot sympathies in Boston as hostages. Gage agreed.

More unpleasant news was in store for the British. A small force of volunteers— the Green Mountain Boys under Ethan Allen—marched to Lake Champlain and struck suddenly at Fort Ticonderoga on May 10, 1775. They caught the British garrison by surprise. Allen rapped with his sword on the door to the commandant's quarters, and cried: "Come out instantly, or I will sacrifice the whole garrison."

A sleepy-eyed captain opened the door.

"I order you instantly to surrender!" Allen shouted.

The British captain blinked. "By what authority do *you* demand a surrender?" he asked.

"In the name of the Great Jehovah and the Continental Congress!" Allen said.

Wisely, the captain accepted Allen's answer and surrendered.

203

WASHINGTON TAKES COMMAND

In Philadelphia, the Continental Congress unanimously selects Washington as commander of its army.

The Continental Congress mentioned by Allen did not actually meet until a few hours later that same day. This Second Congress was held in Philadelphia. As the delegates crowded into the State House (later called Independence Hall) for the opening session, they were confused men. What authority did they truly have? Whom did they really represent? They had no leader, no program of action, no treasury. How could they deal with the problems of war against the mightiest nation on earth?

But the delegates began to speak, and slowly the confusion cleared away. What if the British did destroy their towns and spread ruin along their seacoasts? "These are inconsiderable objects, things of no moment to men whose bosoms glow with the ardor of liberty," they said in one petition to the king.

News that large British reinforcements were arriving in Boston under the command of three new generals—William Howe, Henry Clinton, and "Gentleman Johnny" Burgoyne—swept away the last feelings of hesitation. Clearly, this was a war that might spread to every settlement. Americans must stand together now and form a "Union of Colonies." (At a later session, the name "Union of Colonies" was changed to the "United States of America.") On the motion of John Adams, the militia forces then assembling at Cambridge were named the Continental army. George Washington was unanimously elected commander in chief. On the morning of June 16, 1775, he rose to speak to the congress:

Washington accepted command of the army.

"Though I am truly sensible of the high honor done me . . . yet I feel distress, from a consciousness that my abilities may not be equal to the extensive and important trust. However, as the Congress desire it, I will enter upon the momentous duty, and exert every power I possess in their service, and for the support of the glorious cause. . . .

"As to pay, I beg leave to assure the Congress, that, as no particular consideration could have tempted me to accept this arduous employment, at the expense of my domestic ease and happiness, I do not wish to make any profit from it. I will keep an exact account of my expenses. Those, I doubt not, they will discharge, and that is all I desire."

REBELS ON BREED'S HILL

American troops fortify a height just outside Boston and fight a battle known as the Battle of Bunker Hill.

As Washington journeyed north to take command of his army, he received news of a fierce battle fought outside Boston.

During the night of June 16, the Americans had seized Bunker Hill and Breed's Hill, two heights north of Boston. When the moon rose about midnight, it shed a pale glow on some 1,000 men on Breed's Hill. They were digging furiously to throw up a small fortress and a line of entrenchments. Below them, in the harbor, river, and ferry slip lay four British men-of-war. The ships were so near that the men on the hillside could hear the sentinels on the decks crying, "All's well."

Colonel William Prescott, a farmer from Pepperell with a froglike voice, led the Americans. Most of them, too, were farmers. Their only weapons were the old muskets and fowling pieces they had brought from home, their only ammunition the

The colonial forces worked secretly through the night on Breed's Hill.

small supply of powder and shot they carried in their powder horns and pouches. As the night passed, the earth piled up higher around their little fort. Then a sentinel aboard one of the British ships spotted the men on Breed's Hill and shouted the alarm.

The big guns of the ship, opening the bombardment upon the hillside, awakened Boston. Soon other men-of-war were firing broadsides at the fort which, as if by magic, had sprouted on Breed's Hill during the night. Scrambling out of their beds, Bostonians rushed to the rooftops, balconies, and steeples to watch what was going on. As the sun came up they could see the Americans coolly completing their work with shells bursting about them.

Within Boston, the British generals debated the next move. Howe said that troops should be landed on Charlestown Neck to pinch off any chance of reinforcements reaching the rebels on Breed's Hill. But Gage decided on a direct attack. His reason was easy to guess. These ragtag rebels would run for their lives once they saw British regulars with fixed bayonets marching on them in a solid mass. By noon Gage had loaded his boats with more than 2,000 troops and twelve pieces of cannon.

The men on Breed's Hill watched the boats crossing the Charles River. Weary, hungry, and thirsty, the Americans pleaded for relief, but there was no one to take their place. Israel Putnam, who had walked to Boston with his flock of sheep during the blockade, called on them to stand firm. Seth Pomeroy of Northampton, seventy years of age, encouraged the younger men. Dr. Joseph Warren said calmly: "It is pleasant and becoming to die for one's country."

In the morning, the British were astonished to see their fortifications.

At any rate, there was still work to do. Some of the men crawled to a rail fence behind their unfinished fortifications and wove new-mown hay between the rails to screen themselves from the enemy. Others hid behind haycocks, guns ready.

Some time after three o'clock the great British guns opened fire on the American earthworks. The British advanced in two columns, one under Howe, the other under General Robert Pigot. Behind them the guns on the men-of-war continued to hurl shells at the hillside.

Prescott and his farmers waited quietly. The redcoats came on, puzzled by this silence. But Prescott had ordered his troops not to fire until they could see the whites of the enemy's eyes. No American had to be told that ammunition was scarce and every shot must count. The redcoats were almost upon the fort when the command rang out: "Fire!"

A withering volley ran like flame along the length of the American breastworks. The British reeled, swept away as though a great scythe had mown them down. British blood stained the green slopes of Breed's Hill, and British flags fell among the morning lilies. Other British troops approached what seemed to be a harmless rail fence. They, too, were shot down, and soon bugles sounded, ordering a full retreat.

Standing on a hillside overlooking Breed's Hill, General Burgoyne saw Howe's redcoats racing down the slope. British guns had now set fire to the town of Charlestown, and the steeple of a church was a pyramid of flame above the burning houses. From the surrounding hillsides, spectators watched the battle. Burgoyne later said, "The roar

207

of cannon, mortars and musketry, the crash of churches, . . . whole streets falling in ruins . . . and the reflection that perhaps a defeat was a final loss to the British Empire in America . . . made the whole a picture and a complication of horror and importance beyond anything that ever came to my lot to be witness to."

THE LAST CHARGE

Once more the British attacked. Once more Prescott stood like a rock—sword buckled to his side, a broad-brimmed hat shading his eyes—waiting for the right moment to cry, "Fire!" Once more the redcoats were thrown back.

Howe couldn't believe what was happening. It was, he said, "a moment that I never felt before." But Prescott's ammunition was all but gone. His men had no bayonets with which to stand off the British in a hand-to-hand fight. After two hours of battle, the end was near, and Prescott knew it as the redcoats advanced a third time.

The Americans had no more powder or bullets and fought with the butt ends of their guns. All at once, said Peter Brown, who fought on Breed's Hill that scorching afternoon, the fight of the Americans "went out like an old candle." Peter wrote his mother: "I was in the fort till the regulars came in, and I jumped over the walls and ran for about half a mile where balls flew like hailstones and cannons roared like

Their powder and ammunition gone, the Americans fought with rifle butts and fists.

thunder." The Americans were forced to retreat. Even so, they fought "from one fence or wall to another," as General Burgoyne admitted, and the retreat was "covered with bravery and military skill."

American losses that day were 100 killed, 267 wounded, and 30 taken prisoner. British casualties numbered 1,054. The Battle of Quebec, which had ended the French and Indian War and won England half a continent, had not cost so much. What had the British gained in this battle that was mistakenly called the Battle of Bunker Hill? The British had won little more than a place to pitch their tents. Franklin, writing to English friends, drew another meaning from the battle: "Americans will fight. England has lost her colonies forever."

Making an Army

Washington faces the task of making soldiers out of raw and undisciplined New England farmers.

Washington reached Cambridge, Massachusetts, on July 2, 1775, and the next morning took command of the Continental army. In the following weeks, he had the enormous task of changing farmers into seasoned soldiers. He lacked gunners to handle the few cannon he possessed, but then he lacked almost everything—engineers who could build proper fortifications, ammunition, canvas and sailcloth for tents, money to pay his troops.

Washington found these New England militiamen different from the Virginians who had served under him. They were willing enough to fight, but between battles they wanted to go home and tend to their farms. Washington was used to men who "kept their place" and were respectful to "gentlemen." But New Englanders did not believe in "putting on airs," and a private spoke to a captain as he would to any neighbor.

From the start, discipline was a big problem. Men wandered away from their posts. They used "abusive language" toward officers and fell asleep while on guard duty. Drunkenness and theft were other common offenses for which men were hauled before a military court.

In a letter, Washington made no secret of his dissatisfaction with one class of New England militiamen: "Their officers generally speaking are the most indifferent kind of people I ever saw." He also wrote: "I daresay the men would fight very well (if properly officered) although they are an exceedingly dirty and nasty people." But some of the New Englanders became trusted generals on his staff. Among them were Israel

209

The undisciplined and often disorderly New England soldiers horrified Washington

Putnam, who had been a farmer; Henry Knox, who had been a bookseller in Boston, and Nathanael Greene, the Rhode Island Quaker who became a warrior.

The British sat tight in Boston during the summer and autumn of 1775, and this gave Washington time to whip the easygoing New Englanders into an army. The Reverend William Emerson, who had watched the redcoats at Concord bridge, noticed the change: "Everyone is made to know his place and keep it, or be immediately tied-up, and receive not one but thirty or forty lashes according to his crime," Emerson wrote his wife: "Thousands are at work every day from four till eleven o'clock in the morning. It is surprising the work that has been done. . . ."

With the British strongly entrenched on Bunker Hill, Washington spread his army around them. He was determined to keep the redcoats cooped up on the Boston peninsula and its neighboring islands.

But Howe was willing to wait. Time, he believed, would wear down the colonists' spirit. The long freezing months of winter would also work in his favor. Tired of the cold and their half-empty bellies, the rebels would steal away home and the war would collapse. Nor was Howe altogether wrong. Although the Continental Congress had planned on an army of 20,372 men, divided into regiments of 728 men, enlistments were few. The colonists' leaders could not help wondering how large Washington's army would be when spring came.

ADVENTURE

IN CANADA

An American army marches on Canada, but fails to take Quebec.

Most Canadians were in favor of the American patriots, whom they insisted on calling the Bostonians. An attack on Canada would have a good chance of success, and in the fall of 1775 Washington approved a plan to drive a two-pronged assault into Canada and capture Quebec. Ethan Allen had easily taken Ticonderoga; surely he could do as well again.

And so, in November, Ethan Allen crossed the St. Lawrence River to attack Montreal. But his supporting force failed to reach him, and Allen was captured by the British. They remembered him as the conqueror of Ticonderoga, and they ordered him bound hand and foot with irons. He was thrown into the hold of a warship and left there for five weeks without a seat or a bed.

Meanwhile, a second American force under Colonel Benedict Arnold pushed through the winter snow toward Quebec.

Their food supply ran so low that one night they were forced to kill a dog and make a soup of it. But, in spite of hunger and cold, they went forward. On November 9, 1775, they were near Quebec, which was hidden from them by the falling snow.

Using the cove and ravine Wolfe had discovered sixteen years before, the Americans climbed to the Plains of Abraham. They believed that the friendly people of Quebec would surrender the city as soon as they heard that the Americans had arrived, but news came that an army of Canadians and Indians under Governor Carleton was ready to go into battle. Colonel Arnold, who was no fool, hastily recrossed the river and withdrew to Point aux Trembles (Aspen Trees Point) to await other American forces under Brigadier General Richard Montgomery.

By December the little American army—about 1,000 ill-clothed, ill-fed men—had returned to the Plains of Abraham. They peered through the swirling snow at the walled city, wondering what to do next.

But Montgomery had imagination. He ordered wickerwork baskets filled with snow, over which he poured water. The snow froze into blocks of ice, with which Montgomery soon built a huge mound. On

From his huge, man-made ice mound, Montgomery tried to shell Quebec.

211

it he mounted six twelve-pound cannon and two short cannon called howitzers. A few shells were lobbed into the city before the Canadians fired back. They scored a direct hit on Montgomery's mound, shattering the ice—and the hopes of the Americans.

Other schemes for taking Quebec went no better. Before the year ended, it was plain that the American adventure in Canada was a failure.

WASHINGTON'S FIRST VICTORY

A combination of daring and hard work allows Washington to besiege Boston and drive the British out of the city.

On New Year's Day, "in compliment to the United Colonies," Washington raised a new flag of thirteen red and white stripes with British colors in the upper corner. Spying the strange flag flapping in the breeze on Prospect Hill, the British in Boston believed that Washington wished to surrender. When word of this reached Washington, he smiled. "By this time," he said, "I presume they begin to think it strange that we have not made a formal surrender of our lines."

Washington had no intention of surrendering. He had a plan—a good one—for ousting the British from Boston, but he needed powder and guns to carry it out. Israel Putnam was given the job of getting the powder, and that January a fellow officer wrote: "The bay is open—everything thaws here but Old Put. He is still as hard as ever, crying out for powder—powder—ye gods, give us powder!" Meanwhile, Henry Knox was bringing down the cannon from captured Fort Ticonderoga. Over mountains, through the wilderness that was covered by ice and snow, he hauled the big guns. There were fifty-nine of them, and altogether they weighed 119,900 pounds.

By March Washington had his powder and guns, and had begun to act. For some unknown reason, Howe had failed to seize Dorchester Heights, which overlooked Boston. Washington planned to occupy it. But to keep Howe from learning what he was up to, he bombarded the city from Lechmere's Point, Roxbury, Cobble Hill, Ploughed Hill, and Lamb's Dam. For three

The Americans fortified Dorchester Heights to surprise the British.

days the bombardment went on. Then, at seven o'clock on the night of March 4—the eve of the anniversary of the Boston Massacre—Washington sprang his surprise.

Two thousand men, armed with entrenching tools, swarmed over Dorchester Heights. Three hundred wagons, loaded with fascines (bundles of sticks) and screwed hay (bundles of hay), came in a steady stream. The constant roar of Washington's guns drowned out any sounds made by the men. The weather was cold, the moon full. The long winter night gave the Americans several more hours of darkness to work in than they had had the previous summer, when they had fortified Breed's Hill.

Under Washington's direction two forts were built. Cannon were rolled into position. Barrels filled with stones were placed where they could be rolled down on troops charging up the hill. Trees from nearby orchards were cut down; the logs were sharpened at the ends and thrust into the ground like giant spikes. By daylight, the whole job was finished.

213

When Howe saw what the Americans had accomplished on Dorchester Heights, he was astounded. "I know not what I shall do!" he cried. "The rebels have done more in one night than my whole army would have done in a month."

At a staff meeting that morning, Admiral Shuldham told Howe: "If they retain possession of the Heights, I cannot keep a ship in the harbor." Howe tried to cross the river and storm the Heights, but his troops were beaten back by Washington's cannon, aided by rain and a violent wind. Everything had turned against the redcoats. Despite the protests of terrified Tories, Howe decided to leave Boston without fighting a battle.

The British destroyed all the salt and molasses in the city, wrecked the shops of patriotic merchants, and carried off any linen and woolen goods they could find. They left Boston on March 17. Many Americans must have agreed with the newspaperman who wrote that the British withdrawal was due to "the wisdom, firmness, intrepidity and military abilities of our amiable and beloved general, His Excellency George Washington, Esquire."

A PLOT TO MURDER WASHINGTON

Washington escapes death when he is warned not to eat a plate of poisoned peas.

With Howe forced out of Boston, George III hit upon a new scheme for strengthening his forces in the colonies. He would hire soldiers from other nations to fight his war

One of Washington's guards tried to poison his food.

in America. The rulers of Russia and the Netherlands turned him down. But the princes of some German provinces, particularly Hesse-Cassel, needed money. They agreed to supply George III with about 17,000 Hessian troops. For each soldier, they received $22.50 plus an annual payment. The soldiers themselves were given no choice. They were farmers and laborers, and many of them had been seized for the army while working in their fields or in their shops, or while they were worshiping in church.

Up to this time, George III might have been able to keep his American colonies. A number of the colonists had no wish to break away from England and form their own nation. They were fighting simply to defend their rights as freeborn British subjects. They would have welcomed a compromise with the royal government. But the king made no offer to compromise, and his hiring of the Hessians angered the colonists and brought them a step closer to declaring their independence.

Even so, there were still many colonists who were loyal to the king. These Tories were especially strong in New York City, where they made up a large part of the population. In those days, the city had 25,000 people and was less than a square mile in size. It was squeezed into an area bounded by the East, the Harlem, and the Hudson Rivers. Beyond the city walls were little settlements known as the Bowery, Bloomingdale, and Harlem. Howe saw that New York had great military importance, and on June 30 he arrived at Staten Island with about 10,000 troops. Twelve days later, his brother, Admiral Lord Richard Howe, sailed a large fleet into New York Bay.

Washington, too, knew the importance of New York, and had been bringing troops to the city. By the end of April a number of forts had been built, and Washington added still others. He built Forts Washington and Independence on the northern boundaries of Manhattan Island, and Fort Constitution (later called Fort Lee) across the Hudson River on the New Jersey shore. Meanwhile, his troops enjoyed what one soldier called "some grand Tory rides," adding: "Several of them [Tories] were handled very roughly, being carried through the streets on rails, their clothes tore from their backs and their bodies pretty well mingled with the dust."

The Tories, encouraged by the arrival of the fleet, decided to help their British friends by plotting against George Washington. A soldier named Hickey, one of Washington's guards at his summer headquarters on Richmond Hill, was bribed to persuade a maid to poison a serving of green peas, one of the general's favorite dishes. But the maid revealed the scheme, and Hickey ended up dangling from a rope on the nearby farm of Colonel Henry Rutgers.

215

STEPS TOWARD INDEPENDENCE

The Continental Congress meets in Philadelphia to decide what the colonies should do.

Thomas Paine was an Englishman, the son of a Quaker corset maker. He had worked at various jobs when, in 1774, he met Benjamin Franklin in London. Franklin encouraged him to come to the colonies, and Paine took his advice. Paine was filled with a burning desire for freedom for all men, and in 1776 he wrote a pamphlet entitled *Common Sense,* which sold more than 100,000 copies within several months.

Paine called for American independence, and wrote that "The sun never shone on a worthier cause." His sentences rang like battle cries: "It matters little now what the king of England either says or does. He hath wickedly broken through every moral and human obligation, trampled nature and conscience beneath his feet, and by a steady and constitutional spirit of insolence and cruelty, procured for himself a universal hatred." Paine pleaded with Americans: "A government of our own is our natural right. Ye that love mankind, that dare oppose not only tyranny but the tyrant, stand forth!"

Washington approved Paine's "sound logic, and unanswerable reasoning." So did thousands of other Americans. As they read *Common Sense,* their doubts and hesitation about independence seemed to fade.

On April 22, 1776, North Carolina took the lead in telling its delegates to the Continental Congress "to concur with those in the other colonies in declaring independence." Massachusetts approved the same action next day. Rhode Island and Virginia hedged somewhat, telling their delegates to *propose* independence. Connecticut's delegates were told to *assent* to independence; so were New Hampshire's. New Jersey left the decision to its representatives. Pennsylvania, Georgia, South Carolina, New York, and Delaware took no official action. Maryland at first opposed independence, then swung to Virginia's position.

On June 7, 1776, in the spacious meeting room of the State House in Philadelphia, Richard Henry Lee of Virginia rose to address the Continental Congress. A hush fell over the great hall as in a clear voice he offered the resolution:

"That these United Colonies are, and of right ought to be, free and independent States: and that all political connection between us and the State of Great Britain is, and ought to be, totally dissolved."

John Adams seconded the resolution. To protect Lee and Adams from a British charge of treason, their names were omitted from the official record. John Adams, Benjamin Franklin, Roger Sherman, and Robert Livingston were named to a committee to draw up the Declaration of Independence, but most of the work of drafting the document was done by Thomas Jefferson.

DECLARATION OF INDEPENDENCE

Jefferson worked long hours at a folding desk in the room he had rented at 235 High Street. From his window, as he paced and thought, he looked down on sprawling Philadelphia, broiling in the June heat. Nearby stood a stable, from which came the big green horseflies that were a special bedevilment to Jefferson.

The committee was delighted with Jefferson's statement of why the colonies were declaring their independence. Franklin and Sherman, as far as John Adams could recall, did not "criticize any thing." Adams, for his part, believed that in calling the king a

In a small rented room in Philadelphia, Thomas Jefferson drafted the document that was adopted as the Declaration of Independence.

tyrant Jefferson had made the document "too personal."

They were modest men who met that day in Jefferson's room. As representatives of their colonies, they held only *delegated* power. With time they would see where the *real* power of a free people lay. They would invent a way to make sure this power was felt in government, through popular elections. But this would come later.

Jefferson had written into his Declaration of Independence a hard-hitting paragraph condemning slavery. John Adams knew that the delegates from South Carolina and Georgia would not allow the paragraph to stand. And while New Englanders owned few slaves, Adams knew they too would be touchy on this subject, since their ships had carried slaves to the South for a neat profit.

So, struggling toward freedom, America already was faced with the great themes that would dominate its history. First, there was the conflict between *delegated* power and *real* power. Out of this, free elections and political parties would grow. Secondly, there was the conflict between *material* interests and *moral* interests that even then made the position of the Negro in America something that haunted the minds of men.

For three days, Congress debated the thoughts and language of the Declaration of Independence. As Adams had predicted, the paragraph on slavery was not accepted. Jefferson was annoyed with some of the delegates, who believed "we had friends in England worth keeping terms with." Parts of the Declaration that criticized the people of England were taken out, but the main body of it remained.

In magnificent language, Jefferson stated: "We hold these truths to be self-evident, that all men are created equal, that they are endowed by their Creator with certain unalienable Rights, that among these are Life, Liberty and the pursuit of Happiness." Again he said: ". . . Governments are instituted among Men, deriving their just powers from the consent of the governed. . . ."

faced him in New York. The British fleet under Admiral Howe—"Black Dick," the general's seafaring brother—had forced its way past the American batteries and was threatening Manhattan Island. Washington had placed some 8,000 troops under Israel Putnam on Brooklyn Heights to hold off the redcoats. On August 22, 1776, the British moved on Long Island by land and sea.

The Battle of Long Island was fought five days later, and for the first time Americans went into action against hired Hessian soldiers. A German colonel expressed the contempt of the Hessians for their American foes: "These people ought rather to be pitied than feared. They always require a quarter of an hour to load a rifle, and in the meantime they feel the effects of our balls and bayonets."

A British officer later told why the Hessians behaved so savagely: "We took care to tell the Hessians that the rebels had resolved to give no quarter to them in particular, which made them fight desperately, and put all to death that fell into their hands."

Among the Americans who fought on Long Island was fifteen-year-old Joseph Plumb Martin, a farm lad from Massachusetts who was eager to "sniff a little gunpowder." Near the ferry dock, on the Manhattan side of the East River, he loaded his knapsack from the casks of sea bread provided for the troops and then marched aboard the transport.

When they landed on the Brooklyn shore, young Martin saw that the Americans were taking terrific punishment. Wounded men streamed past him, "some with broken arms, some with broken legs, and some with broken heads." To lift his spirits, Martin gnawed on his sea bread and found it "hard enough to break the teeth of a rat."

On July 4, 1776, the Declaration of Independence was adopted by the colonies. Four days later the document was read to Philadelphians, who burst into loud cheers. Next day New Yorkers, cheering the Declaration, marched to Bowling Green and pulled down the statue of the king; later they used the lead to make 40,000 bullets. Washington's troops held a celebration, almost forgetting the British fleet off Manhattan Island.

DISASTER ON LONG ISLAND

The Hessians take Long Island and Washington orders his men to retreat.

While news of the Declaration of Independence traveled through the colonies and was celebrated in one town after another, Washington worried over the problem that

The call came, "Fall in!" Heart thumping, Martin fell into line. Soon the regiment moved forward toward a creek. Driven into the muddy water, the men thrashed wildly, some swimming, some sinking from view. From a hilltop British fieldpieces poured death upon the outnumbered Americans "like a shower of hail." An American twelve-pounder, opening up, made the redcoats hop for cover.

Martin later recalled the plight of a regiment of Maryland volunteers: "When they came out of the water and mud to us, looking like water rats, it was a truly pitiful sight. Many of them were killed in the pond and more were drowned. Some of us went into the water after the fall of the tide, and took out a number of corpses and a great many arms that were sunk in the pond and creek."

Washington was heard to exclaim: Good God! What brave fellows I must this day lose!" And lose them he did—about 1,000 in all. The British force curled around him, crumbling his left flank and piercing the center of his lines. He was pushed into a little corner of the island less than two miles square. One British force was in front of him. A naval force with 20,000 redcoats was behind him.

The men who saw Washington that day, riding his big gray horse, could tell by the dark circles under his eyes that he had gone without sleep for many hours. Yet his mind remained alert, his military judgment sound. It seemed impossible now to snatch men, guns, equipment, and stores from under Howe's blazing guns. But Washington managed to do it, and retreat safely back across the East River to New York. Luck was with him. A Negro servant sent by a Tory lady to tell Howe of the crossing fell into the hands of Hessians. They could not understand a word the poor fellow said. Too late, Howe learned that he had been outwitted.

The Battle of Long Island and Washington's retreat to White Plains

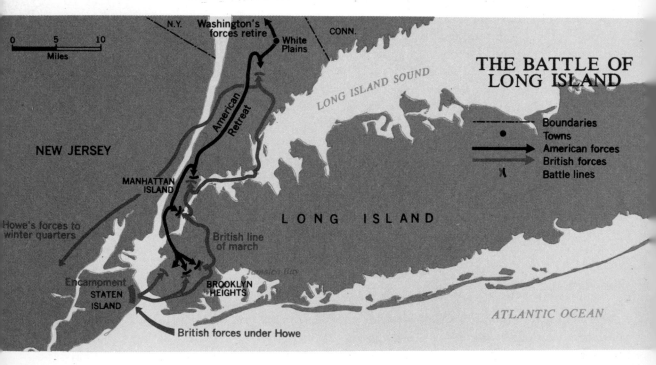

The Americans fought bitterly as they tried to escape the British guns.

ON HARLEM HEIGHTS

A peace conference fails, and Washington moves his headquarters from Harlem to a position close to White Plains.

Now that the Americans had been beaten on Long Island, Admiral Howe felt that this was the right time to offer them peace terms. In September he met on Staten Island with John Adams, Benjamin Franklin, and Edward Rutledge, the American peace commission. The admiral refused to accept either the authority of Congress or the independence of the colonies. Politely but firmly, the Americans ended the peace talks: "You may call us what you please. We are, nevertheless, the representatives of a free and independent people, and will entertain no proposition which does not recognize our independence."

These were unhappy weeks for Washington. Retreats, no matter how skillfully carried out, do not win wars, and the people

221

had much to grumble about. In New York, which had many Tories, the army was behaving badly, plundering houses and annoying residents. Stories were told of surgeons who sold furloughs to able-bodied men for sixpence each. Drunkenness was common. Many people felt that what the army needed most was a new commander.

NATHAN HALE IS HANGED

Washington ordered an issue of two days' supply of bread and pork to all his troops, proof that he might be forced to march at any moment. His position in New York City was risky, and in September he drew his army north to Harlem Heights. Badly in need of information on what the British would do next, he sent a trusted captain, Nathan Hale, to act as a spy in the enemy's camp.

Captain Hale entered the British encampment dressed as a farmer. He had been making sketches and notes for Washington when a Tory relative recognized him. Betrayed by a member of his own family, Hale calmly accepted his death sentence as a spy. In the morning when young Hale stood beneath a tree, a rope around his neck, spectators crowding around him broke into sobs. According to legend, Hale then spoke these last words: "I only regret that I have but one life to lose for my country."

For almost a month Washington waited on Harlem Heights for General Howe to make a move. His entrenchments were strong—especially Fort Washington, rising 235 feet above the tidewater of the Hudson, and Fort Lee, perched across the river on the high cliffs of New Jersey. From the beginning, as Washington confessed in a letter to Congress, he was troubled. Would his troops, still shaken after the disastrous and exhausting Battle of Long Island, stand up to another assault?

On October 12, Howe used ninety flat-

boats to carry a large part of his army to Throg's Neck, a low peninsula that juts out from what is today New York's Borough of the Bronx. A brisk skirmish forced him to take to the heights of New Rochelle. Here, squarely across the road leading to the little village of White Plains, Howe was joined by a number of newly arrived Hessian troops.

Washington moved swiftly, knowing it was time to get off Manhattan Island. Leaving a garrison at Fort Washington, he

David Bushnell hoped to attack British ships in New York harbor from his one-man submarine, the Turtle, *but the idea proved unsuccessful and was given up.*

marched his army up the valley of the Bronx River. Along the heights from Fordham to White Plains the Americans pitched their camps. Every day brought bitter skirmishing. Washington reached White Plains and set up headquarters on high ground to the north of the village. He had chosen a strong defensive position. His restlessness showed that he shared the feelings of the men in the ranks. General and private alike knew that they would soon be engaged in battle.

Race across
New Jersey

Fort Washington falls, and British and American troops race for Philadelphia.

The fighting at White Plains rose to furious pitch on October 28. The key to the battle was Chatterton's Hill, across the Bronx River, where the Americans were already

From Fort Lee, on the New Jersey side of the Hudson, Washington and Thomas Paine watched Fort Washington fall to the British.

entrenched. Redcoats and Hessians splashed across the river and up the hill. Artillery raked Washington's entrenchments.

Step by step the Americans gave way, and losing Chatterton's Hill amounted to losing the battle. For days the armies rested within a "long cannon shot" of each other, but Washington knew he must retreat. Rain and wind swept White Plains as the Americans withdrew on November 10.

Washington now had to sprinkle his forces like salt from a shaker. To guard the New York highlands, he sent troops to Peekskill, about eighteen miles above White Plains. Some 7,000 soldiers under General Charles Lee were stationed at North Castle, where they could be called into action when needed. Washington and about 2,000 troops withdrew across the river to Fort Lee.

Even lazy General Howe understood that there was little to keep him from moving through New Jersey to Philadelphia, the seat of the Continental Congress. Howe planned first to storm the American garrison still in Fort Washington. This task he assigned to Scottish Highlander and Hessian troops. In the British general's hands were sketches and reports brought to him by William Demont, a Pennsylvania adjutant turned deserter.

Things were going badly for the small American garrison at Fort Washington. Demont told of the bickering between officers and privates, and the lack of ammunition, food, and clothing. The Highlanders and Hessians attacked vigorously, meeting stiffer opposition than they had expected. But in the end swamps were waded, cliffs scaled, and the earthworks broken through.

The cold, tattered, hungry Americans who fell prisoner amused the British, and

one of their officers wrote: "Their odd fig-

ures frequently excited the laughter of our soldiers." But there was nothing amusing to an American about the British prison ships, like the *Jersey*. Rancid food, foul air, filth, and vermin were only some of the horrors suffered by the prisoners in the *Jersey's* hold. The living, the dying, and the dead lay huddled together. Each sundown brought the same cry: *"Down,* rebels, down!" And each morning was announced by the same brutal shout: "Rebels, turn out your dead!"

FORT LEE ABANDONED

Washington watched the collapse of Fort Washington from the New Jersey shore. Beside him stood Thomas Paine, the author of *Common Sense*. Fort Lee could not be held now. Washington's only choice was a race with the British across New Jersey toward Philadelphia. General Charles Lee must leave North Castle on the Croton River and quickly bring his forces across the Hudson to Washington's support, and New Jersey citizens must rally to the patriots' cause.

The race between Washington's straggling army and a powerful British force under General Charles Cornwallis began at the little Dutch village of Hackensack. It went on through Newark, New Brunswick, Princeton, and Trenton. The people of New Jersey seemed to lose their patriotism whenever Cornwallis appeared. They almost fell over one another in their eagerness to safeguard their property by swearing oaths of allegiance to the royal government.

"We seem to be playing at Bo-Peep," said a British officer. If the race across New Jersey was a game, it was a frantic one for the ragged Continentals who often marched through freezing rains without stockings and shoes. At each town Washington waited until the redcoats were almost upon him. Where was Lee? Hourly, the question

tormented Washington: "Lee—why doesn't Lee come?" But that strange individual, who had sneered at Washington as "not a heaven-born genius," ambled into New Jersey as if he had all the time in the world. In mid-December he rested in the little mountain village of Basking Ridge, still miles away from his hard-pressed commander in chief. There one day, while Lee was loitering in the local tavern, writing a letter, the British swooped down and captured him.

Bagging Lee added to the cheer of the British as Christmas approached. On December 8, a force of 6,000 redcoats under General Henry Clinton overran Rhode Island and settled around Newport. On that same frosty Sunday, the advance guard of Cornwallis' army entered Trenton, just as the rear guard of Washington's forces was crossing the Delaware River.

Panic swept Philadelphia. The Continental Congress prepared to flee to Baltimore. In those dark hours a new pamphlet by Thomas Paine, *The American Crisis*, again raised the spirits of the Americans. Paine wrote:

"These are the times that try men's souls. The summer soldier and the sunshine patriot will, in this crisis, shrink from the service of his country; but he that stands it NOW, deserves the love and thanks of man and woman. Tyranny, like Hell, is not easily conquered; yet we have this consolation with us, that the harder the conflict, the more glorious the triumph."

Washington landed at Trenton in sleet and freezing rain.

TRENTON—"VICTORY OR DEATH"

Washington crosses the Delaware and takes the Hessians by surprise.

"I will not despair," Washington had muttered on leaving New Brunswick. Now, pacing his headquarters in Pennsylvania, he was preparing a surprise for the Hessians under Colonel Johann Rall, who occupied Trenton. Two days before Christmas, Washington ordered rations cooked for three days. The password which he gave his sentries was "Victory or Death."

Washington was gambling on the German habit of holding a big celebration on Christmas Day. The Hessians would drink vast quantities of beer and dance far into the night. Morning would find them drowsy, muddleheaded, careless. It would be the perfect time for an attack.

At twilight on Christmas night Washington's men began boarding boats at McConky's Ferry, a few miles above Trenton. A wintry wind blew, and masses of ice floated in the Delaware River. A swift cur-

227

rent swept the ice cakes against the boats. Toward midnight snow began to fall.

"I never have seen Washington so determined as he is now," Colonel John Fitzgerald wrote in his diary at three o'clock that morning. "He stands on the bank of the river, wrapped in his cloak, superintending the landing of his troops. The storm is changing to sleet and cuts like a knife. The last cannon is being landed, and we are ready to mount our horses."

THE DEFEAT OF THE HESSIANS

Grimly, the American army marched on Trenton. At eight o'clock, when Colonel Rall was still sleeping off the wine he had drunk the night before, Washington's forces struck. The Continentals quickly overran the town and gained possession of the road to Princeton. Part of the vigorous action was led by Lieutenant James Monroe, a future President of the United States. Rall pulled off his nightshirt, put on a uniform, and tried to rally his flustered troops. It was too late. At noon that December 26, 1776, Colonel Fitzgerald wrote in his diary:

"His men [the Hessians] were frightened and confused, for our men were firing upon them from fences and houses and they were falling fast. Instead of advancing they ran into an apple orchard." The path of retreat toward Bordentown was cut off and by noon Washington had collected nearly 1,000 prisoners, six cannon, over 1,000 muskets, twelve drums, and four stands of colors. Colonel Fitzgerald could not conceal his admiration for Washington. He wrote:

"It is a glorious victory. It will rejoice the hearts of our friends everywhere and give new life to our hitherto waning fortunes. Washington has baffled the enemy in his retreat from New York. He has pounced upon the Hessians like an eagle upon a hen and is safe once more on this side of the river. If he does nothing more, he will live in history as a great military commander."

WASHINGTON BEDEVILS THE BRITISH

Washington takes Princeton, then settles his tired army in Morristown for the winter.

It was not a happy New Year's Day for General Cornwallis. He had planned to return to England for a vacation. Instead, he found himself riding from New York to Princeton to take personal command of the British forces. The redcoats now numbered about 8,000, while Washington had 5,000 footsore, hungry men at Trenton. Rain turned the roads into bogs of mud as Cornwallis plunged on toward Trenton, determined to smash Washington forever.

But Washington's riflemen, striking unexpectedly in brisk little skirmishes, made

Cornwallis' march a constant misery. Meanwhile, Washington had decided on a bold move. He would march by a roundabout road and hit suddenly at the British reserves and stores of supplies at Princeton.

Washington's surprise appearance threw the redcoats into confusion. The British retreated into the building of the College of New Jersey (now Princeton University) and were promptly bombarded by an American cannon. After two or three shots the redcoats hung a white flag out the window.

The Battle of Princeton was over in less than an hour. Washington had been in the thick of it, riding a white horse. The prisoners who fell into American hands were described as "a haughty, crabbed set of men." Washington told his staff gaily: "It is a fine fox to chase, my boys."

Cornwallis now fell back to New Brunswick to protect his post there. Washington withdrew into the mountains near Morris-town, content to settle down for the winter.

Huts began to dot the countryside as the ragged Americans fought off the chill winds and blustering snow squalls. There were many desertions and few enlistments, so that Washington could almost see his army melting away. Smallpox spread through the camp. It was difficult to tell which the men feared more—the disease or the inoculations Washington ordered.

Yet brighter times were ahead. New Jersey citizens, who had so willingly taken oaths of allegiance to the royal government, now began to support the patriots. They had discovered that the Hessians made no distinction between foe and friend. Houses were broken into, families were robbed of food and clothes, and even young children and old people were shamefully mistreated.

The people of New Jersey daily grew more rebellious against their so-called British protectors. Now they gave any informa-

A surprise attack on Princeton forced the British to retreat into a college building.

Martha Washington joined her husband in Morristown, sharing the discomforts of army life so that she could spend the winter with the "Old Man."

tion they could to American horsemen, who spent the good winter days raiding enemy outposts. By the first of March the British and Hessians had drawn back into their strongholds at New Brunswick and Amboy. Washington's riders were "cleaning up" the New Jersey countryside.

In the pleasant little village of Morristown life was not all war and worry for the commander in chief. One day a coach brought a woman "so plainly dressed" that bystanders believed she must be a servant. But she was Martha Washington, and Washington greeted her warmly. She had arrived to spend the winter with the "Old Man," as she affectionately called him.

In "elegant silks and ruffles," the ladies of Morristown visited Mrs. Washington, who received them in "a speckled homespun apron" while knitting a stocking. Polite and smiling, Martha Washington was setting an example of how women must help to win the war by doing without anything they could not make for themselves.

Throughout the winter, the army nipped at the foe. A raid on a British schooner at Elizabethtown supplied badly needed blankets, and a hit-and-run assault on Spanktown (later called Rahway) produced about 1,000 bushels of salt. As spring came, the first of 8,000 fresh American troops reached Morristown, and Washington prepared once more to battle the redcoats.

Even the warm weather did not tempt Howe to leave the gay social life of New York. Surprisingly, one of Howe's closest companions was the captured American, General Charles Lee. Lee obligingly worked out a plan for the British to seize Philadelphia, Annapolis, and Alexandria, and divide the colonies north and south.

By late May, Washington decided to move down to the first range of the Watchung Mountains, about seven miles from New Brunswick, to counter any move the British might make. But not until June was half over did Howe turn his attention back to the war, and a series of little sparring matches developed between the two armies before the new campaign took shape.

Howe's aim was to lure Washington out of his mountain stronghold, but Washington was too wise to fall into that trap. In July Howe loaded his troops onto British vessels, leaving Washington to guess his intentions. Patriot spies on Staten Island were as mystified as Washington as to which way Howe would move—north or south.

RED FLOWS THE BRANDYWINE

Defeated on the banks of the Brandywine, Washington retreats, leaving Philadelphia to Howe.

In early August, Washington learned that Howe's vessels were sailing into Chesapeake Bay. It was clear that Howe intended to land somewhere around Wilmington, Delaware, and then swing his columns north to capture Philadelphia.

With recently arrived reinforcements, Washington's forces now totaled about 16,000 men. He was cheered by news of a thumping American victory to the north at Bennington, up in "the New Hampshire Grants" (Vermont), where Americans had routed a British force commanded by two of Burgoyne's officers. And Washington recently had found a new friend—the nineteen-year-old Marquis de Lafayette, who had come from France to offer his services as a soldier without pay.

HOWE OUTWITS WASHINGTON

Washington started after Howe. He reached Philadelphia and treated its citizens to a display of American military strength. On Sunday, August 24, the American army marched in a three-hour parade—down Front Street, up Chestnut, a turn at the common, then across Middle Ferry to the heights of Darby. Washington's orders were to march in step "without *dancing* along." Twelve deep, the men swung through Philadelphia, but John Adams was not altogether pleased. He said, "They don't hold up their heads quite erect, nor turn out their toes so exactly as they ought."

But dress parades do not win wars. Washington's problem was to stop Howe from taking Philadelphia. Moving to Brandywine Creek, about seven or eight miles northwest of Wilmington, he placed his troops with great skill. Howe could not reach Philadelphia without crossing the Brandywine, and now Washington's troops covered a two-mile stretch of that stream. The center of the American line was at Chadd's Ford, where the British could be expected to try to cross.

Howe had many faults. He was slow, liked personal pleasure too much, and was often overconfident. But he was not stupid. 231

The Battle of Brandywine, opening at daybreak on September 11, 1777, found Howe launching a frontal attack on Washington's strong position at Chadd's Ford.

Too late, Washington discovered he had been tricked. The frontal attack was a bluff. Troops under Cornwallis had taken a road to the left in a long, rapid march. By two o'clock they were across the Brandywine, attacking the Continentals from behind.

When Washington awoke to the bitter truth, he had to pull back his forces to meet the British threat. The result was not very happy. A British officer described the action: "There was a most infernal fire of cannon and musquetry, a most incessant shouting, 'Incline to the right! Incline to the left! Halt! Charge!' etc. The balls plowing up the ground. The trees cracking over one's head."

Washington's losses were between 1,200 and 1,300 killed, wounded, and missing. Those of the British numbered only eighty-nine killed, 488 wounded. More American blood than British had stained the Brandywine red that day. Lafayette, shot in the leg, wrapped a bandage around the wound and helped Washington pull his army back in good order.

Howe pushed on toward Philadelphia, crossed the Schuylkill River, and on September 26 occupied the city. He had bagged a real prize. The city's residents did not seem disturbed by the British. Indeed, Washington grumbled that they gave Howe information the Americans had never received.

Washington waited his chance to spring at Howe, who had camped at Germantown, some seven miles northwest of Philadelphia. With his own army strung along the hills a dozen miles away, Washington could guess what Howe wanted—possession of the Delaware River, so that supplies could be brought to Philadelphia by water.

Again Washington planned a surprise. On the night of October 3 he sent his men down all four roads leading into the village of Germantown. From the start the American plan was faulty. Seven miles separated the four roads, so that each part of the army never knew what the other three were doing. A heavy fog added to the confusion.

The center of the battle found one American brigade mistaking another for the British. Americans began firing on Americans, but in the panic that followed, Washington once more managed an orderly retreat.

American losses, including prisoners, were 1,100, twice what Howe had suffered.

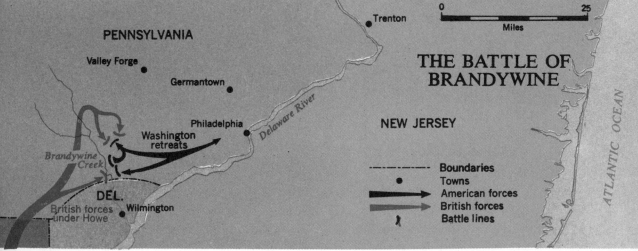

Washington was outflanked by Howe and defeated in the Battle of Brandywine.

1777

Although wounded in the leg, Lafayette rallied his troops against the British attack.

THE DOWNFALL OF GENTLEMAN JOHNNY

After taking Fort Ticonderoga, Burgoyne is defeated at Bennington and Saratoga, where he surrenders.

British General John Burgoyne had taken part in driving the Americans from Canada during the campaign of Montgomery and Arnold in 1775 and 1776. Then Gentleman Johnny had returned to England, where he had talked himself into high favor with the king.

Burgoyne got what he wanted—an army to command. But his orders were strict. He was to do one thing only. Driving down from Canada, he was to push into the Hudson Valley and join with Howe's forces moving up the river.

Burgoyne had ideas of his own about the fighting abilities of Americans. Give the Yankee farmers a tree or stone wall or rail fence to hide behind, he said, and they fought fairly well. But in a great pitched battle they would fall apart.

Gentleman Johnny started from Canada to lay siege to Fort Ticonderoga, his first objective. Here some 3,500 Americans under General Arthur St. Clair, well warned of Burgoyne's advance, had been busily building Fort Independence on the east shore of Lake Champlain as an added defense. But in front of old Fort Ti stood Sugar Hill, key to the whole American position. It was undefended, for St. Clair did not understand its importance.

Burgoyne did. He dragged a cannon into position on the hilltop and sent St. Clair's troops scampering into the Green Mountains. Part of the loot which the British collected with the capture of Fort Ti was 128 American cannon.

Burgoyne was equally sure that final success was merely a question of time. Faced now with choosing an easy passage across Lake George or pursuing the Americans through dense forests, Burgoyne decided to go by land.

Twenty days of chopping through the woods brought his army only twenty miles to the upper waters of the Hudson River, near Fort Edward. Burgoyne would not think of sitting down to dinner, even in the wilderness, without his bottle of wine, and he needed thirty wagons to carry his personal belongings.

A month at Fort Edward left Gentleman Johnny in a sad fix. He had counted on Tories of the region to supply his army, but most of the people were openly unfriendly.

After seizing Forts Ticonderoga and Edward, Burgoyne's armies were beaten back at Bennington (Vermont) and finally forced to surrender at Saratoga, New York.

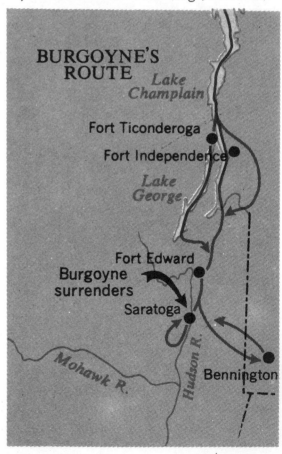

BURGOYNE'S ROUTE

Lake Champlain

Fort Ticonderoga

Fort Independence

Lake George

Fort Edward

Burgoyne surrenders

Saratoga

Mohawk R.

Hudson R.

Bennington

His army faced starvation. Even the hay for his horses had to be hauled in from Canada.

But Burgoyne remembered his strict orders. He decided to push on to meet Howe. (It happened that, at that moment, Howe was on his ship moving south to tangle with Washington for possession of Philadelphia.) Burgoyne then heard that there were mountains of provisions stored at Bennington, a town about twenty-five miles east of the Hudson River—and he badly needed food.

By now Gentleman Johnny appeared to have a talent for doing the wrong thing. Not only did he decide to make the difficult march to Bennington, but he also selected for the expedition 600 Hessians. These were the troops New Englanders hated most. They called them "hired killers" and were sure to fight them fiercely.

THE BATTLES OF BENNINGTON AND SARATOGA

In command of the militiamen from the New Hampshire Grants was rugged old John Stark. This tall, blue-eyed farmer had fought from Bunker Hill to Trenton, then had stomped home when Congress failed to raise his military rank. Now back in service, Stark especially disliked the Hessians.

Burgoyne counted on taking Bennington by surprise, but on August 16, 1777, his troops found Stark's boys dug in and ready for them. The Battle of Bennington was a slaughter. A second American force slipped behind the Hessians and they were caught between two fires. Burgoyne threw in 500 reinforcements but they too were chopped down, bringing the British losses for the day to about 800. The Americans lost seventy men. Staggered by this beating, Burgoyne drew back to Saratoga.

Quickly an American force under General Benjamin Lincoln moved in, cut off Burgoyne's communications with Canada, and attacked Fort Ticonderoga. Isolated on the west bank of the Hudson River, Bur-

General John Burgoyne

235

goyne was now met by a strong American force under General Horatio Gates. Gates wore thick-lensed glasses, and some of his men called him "old grandmother." He was no Washington. Cranky and petty, he quarreled with almost everyone. Yet his position outside Saratoga was strong, and there he waited for Burgoyne to attack.

Gentleman Johnny, with his line of retreat to Canada cut, had to move or perish. He threw his force against the Americans in a furious assault on September 19. Daniel Morgan, using a turkey call to rally his Virginia riflemen, opened fire from behind the trees of a dense woods. Burgoyne's redcoats fell back, with Morgan's boys howling at their heels. Thus began the battle in which, as one general said, "both armies seemed determined to conquer or die." In the end Burgoyne failed to break out of his trap. His losses came to about 500.

Burgoyne prayed for reinforcements, for he knew that he would have to fight again. The reinforcements never came, but the Americans were having their troubles too. Gates had quarreled with Benedict Arnold. As a result, Arnold resigned his commission as a colonel, but remained on the field when Burgoyne struck once more on October 7.

As a volunteer, Arnold leaped on an iron-gray horse, and one Connecticut soldier believed that he behaved "more like a madman than a cool and discreet soldier." That day Arnold was everywhere—fighting now with Morgan, now with two brigades crashing through the center of the line, now with some Massachusetts regiments routing the Hessians from a pair of stockaded cabins. He fought wildly until a bullet struck his leg and ended his furious one-man war.

By then Burgoyne's army had been torn apart. He retired again to Saratoga, but American sharpshooters gave him no rest. Surrounded by the constant threat of death, deserted by the last of his Indian allies, his food gone and his army beaten, Gentleman Johnny surrendered on October 17, 1777.

ORDEAL AT VALLEY FORGE

The army survives a brutal winter and in spring drills under General von Steuben.

A thirteen-cannon salute was fired in Washington's camp to celebrate the American victory at Saratoga. A little skirmish with Howe at White Marsh next day ended the fighting for 1777. On December 17, Washington marched his tired and ragged army into the bleak hills at Valley Forge, twenty miles from Philadelphia. Both the Continental Congress (which had withdrawn to the little town of York) and the

legislature of Pennsylvania then protested Washington's decision to build a winter encampment for his weary troops. Let him keep fighting and drive Howe from Philadelphia, the legislators said, as they warmed themselves before comfortable fireplaces.

Many people criticized Washington at this time. They said he made a habit of failure, and pointed out his defeats at Long Island, White Plains, Brandywine, and Germantown. They called him a dictator, a self-appointed king, a military incompetent. They agreed with the attorney general of Pennsylvania, who said, "Thousands of lives and millions [of dollars] of property are yearly sacrificed to the insufficiency of our Commander-in-Chief. Two battles he has lost for us by two such blunders as might have disgraced a soldier of three months' standing, and yet we are so attracted to this man that I fear we shall rather sink with him than throw him off our shoulders."

The attorney general was one of a group of men who were plotting with some army officers to get rid of Washington as commander in chief. Most of the group were New Englanders who wanted to win back control of the army and American politics. Among the conspirators was General Thomas Conway, a soldier of fortune who had joined the American army, and the plotters became known as the Conway Cabal (secret association). The plot failed, and Washington was in an even stronger position than he was before.

After two years as commander in chief,

During the harsh winter at Valley Forge, the American army was badly clothed and almost always hungry. Before spring came, 2,500 men had died.

Washington needed no one to tell him the problems of the Continental army. With the thirteen colonies behaving like thirteen separate nations, the Continental Congress was not a very effective legislative body. It had no power to tax, and the paper money it issued had so little value that a wagonload of it was needed to buy a wagonload of provisions. The army lacked decent clothing. Its weapons were often so crude that Benjamin Franklin suggested giving the soldiers bows and arrows, since a man could shoot four arrows as fast as one bullet. Powder and lead for bullets were scarce. Just as scarce was the paper needed as wadding for ramming powder and ball into muskets. To get paper, the soldiers tore apart German Bibles they found in Pennsylvania.

These were a few of the problems on Washington's mind as he watched his shivering soldiers build huts for their winter camp at Valley Forge. Blood from their bare feet sometimes stained the snow as they worked. Washington said that it was much easier to criticize "in a comfortable room by a good fireside, than to occupy a cold, bleak hill, and sleep under frost and snow without clothes or blankets." He watched sick men die because there was not even straw to protect them from the wet, cold ground. He wrote unhappily: "From my soul I pity these miseries which is neither in my power to relieve or prevent."

The wintry days at Valley Forge fell into a grim pattern. At mealtime, when soldiers asked what they could eat, the usual answer was: "Fire cake and water." "Fire cake" was a bread baked on a fire without an oven. It was soggy and tasteless. The surprising fact was not that some men deserted from Valley

Although the suffering was great, surprisingly few soldiers deserted.

General von Steuben was an experienced German officer who came to America and joined Washington's staff. He was given the job of drilling and disciplining the raw Colonial troops. Although he shouted and swore at his men, they respected him and obeyed his orders.

Forge, but that so many stayed. "No pay, no clothes, no provisions, no rum," the soldiers sang out, but they seldom blamed Washington. They looked up to him, and it was he who held the army together that winter.

Spring found its way along the banks of the Schuylkill and into the hills at Valley Forge. Since February there had been a new member on Washington's staff, Baron Friedrich Wilhelm Ludolf Gerhard Augustin von Steuben. He was an old German soldier who knew how to drill discipline into an army. Stout, big-nosed, his head almost bald, he strode before the troops with a greyhound loping at his heels.

He would drill these ragged troops until they were as fine as any fighting force in the world—and drill them he did, day in and day out, with his bright eyes glittering Sometimes he swore at the men in German, sometimes in French, and sometimes in both languages. When even this failed to get results, he shouted to an aide: "Come and swear for me in English. These fellows won't do what I bid them."

In time, they did as he asked. They came to understand the baron's affection for them and grinned at his roaring outbursts. Soon they were standing, marching, wheeling as soldiers should.

239

In contrast to Valley Forge, the British spent a pleasant winter in Philadelphia.

BAD NEWS FOR THE BRITISH

After Burgoyne's defeat, the American representatives in Paris persuade the French to enter the war.

During the months of suffering at Valley Forge, Howe and his troops lived comfortably in Philadelphia. A few rugged rebels taunted the soldiers by singing patriotic songs like *War and Washington* and *Burgoyne's Defeat*. But there were many loyalists in the city who shared in the gay times of the invaders. Three times a week British officers and loyalists attended plays performed by an amateur theatrical group. There were elegant dances and dinners, and gambling at the gaming tables. "You can have no idea of the life of continued amusement I live in," wrote one of the many Tory ladies of Philadelphia.

Although the British still had the upper hand, the Americans were about to gain new strength. Their warmest friend in Europe was Count Charles de Vergennes, the French foreign minister. Vergennes looked upon England as a "greedy" neighbor and "the natural enemy of France." Since the closing weeks of 1776, Benjamin Franklin, Silas Deane, and Arthur Lee had been in France, trying to persuade the French gov-

had become the first European power to recognize the United States as an independent nation. America now had a strong ally.

These were unhappy days in London. The dreadful defeat of Burgoyne had been a blow at British pride, and Howe, wasting the winter in Philadelphia, aroused scornful criticism. Knowing that a French fleet and French troops would soon come to the aid of America, the British had to change their plans. Philadelphia would have to be abandoned in favor of New York. New York was an island and would be easier to defend against a land and naval assault.

The British government needed someone to blame for all these misfortunes, and on May, 1778, Howe was replaced as commander by Sir Henry Clinton. The men in Howe's army were shocked by the change. Even more shocked were the Tories, who wondered what would happen to them when their British protectors left Philadelphia. Their gay times were over; there was trouble ahead.

GUNS ROAR
AT MONMOUTH

Replacing the incompetent Lee, Washington is victorious at the Battle of Monmouth.

ernment to make an open alliance with America. With Washington driven first from New York and then from Philadelphia, France was cautious. She was willing to help "secretly." She would send ammunition and allow American privateers that raided British shipping to use her ports. But an open break with England seemed too risky.

When Gentleman Johnny surrendered at Saratoga, the situation changed. A British army had been defeated! Now was the time to strike, while England was floundering. The French government signed a treaty of friendship with America on February 6, 1778. The following month, the French ambassador in London announced that France

On June 18, the British army marched out of Philadelphia. Thousands of desperate Tories fled with Clinton's soldiers. Carrying what few personal belongings they could, the Tories trudged from the city. Tears ran down their cheeks, for they were leaving homes they loved. But, fearing the American troops who would surely re-enter the city, they preferred broken hearts to broken necks.

In charge of the American occupation forces in Philadelphia was Benedict Arnold, 241 whose bravery had raised him to the rank of general. Arnold moved into the mansion where Howe had lived, and provided himself with a housekeeper, a coachman, a groom, and seven other servants. Soon he was living like a king. He gave extravagant dinners, rode through the streets in a handsome coach, and courted pretty, blonde Peggy Shippen. Peggy's tastes, like Arnold's, were expensive. Moreover, she was a well-known Tory. But Arnold did not seem to care. He married the headstrong Peggy, meanwhile piling up debts. He was falling into a trap that would make him forever remembered in history.

As the redcoats and Hessians under Clinton crossed the Delaware River and marched through New Jersey toward Sandy Hook, another American general was giving Washington trouble. No one had worked harder than Washington to gain Charles Lee's freedom. Washington respected Lee's abilities and had placed him second in command of the forces pursuing Clinton. Lee was a professional soldier who had fought in Portugal, Poland, Turkey, and Hungary. He looked on Washington as only an amateur, and believed himself a far better judge of how Clinton and his forces should be handled.

Even though a cannon ball ripped her skirt, Mary Hayes continued to bring water to the American cannoneers, and became known as "Molly Pitcher."

Cannon helped win the Battle of Monmouth.

Clinton's march across New Jersey was a difficult one. The roads twisted through forests, and every mile was a misery. Bridges were down and trees had been felled to block his passage. The British were also hampered by a train of supply wagons that stretched for twelve miles. When the British reached the Raritan River and turned southeastward toward Sandy Hook, the baggage train cut Clinton's forces in two.

On Sunday, June 28, with a sweltering sun beating down, Washington saw a chance to fall on the rear half of Clinton's army. The redcoats were moving over difficult country toward Monmouth Court House (Freehold). Washington sent repeated orders ahead to Lee—attack, attack! Lee failed to act, and Washington, pushing on to the front, found to his astonishment that the British, not the Americans, were on the offensive.

Lee tried to explain why he had not followed Washington's orders. "Sir," he said, "these troops are not able to meet British grenadiers."

Washington's temper exploded. "Sir," he said, "they are able, and, by God, they shall do it!"

Washington took command. He braced himself to halt the retreat of the confused and disorganized Americans, who were being chased by the British troops. A narrow road, passing through swampy land, gave him a spot to cut off the British assault. His cannoneers rolled up their guns and fired at the redcoats.

Men carried away different memories of the rip-roaring Battle of Monmouth that blistering Sunday, depending on where they fought. One man remembered Washington's calmness: "After passing us, he rode on to the plain [level] field and took an observation of the advancing enemy. He remained there some time upon his old English charger, while the shot from the British artillery were rendering up the earth all around him."

Another man remembered Mary Ludwig Hayes, who carried water to the American cannoneers: "While in the act of reaching a cartridge and having one of her feet as far before the other as she could step, a cannon shot from the enemy passed directly between her legs, without doing any other damage than carrying away all the lower part of her petticoat." History renamed Mary Hayes and made a legend of her as "Molly Pitcher."

Wrapped in his cloak, Washington slept on the ground with his troops that night, expecting the battle to begin again at daybreak. But Clinton had had enough. Abandoning his badly wounded and leaving his dead unburied, he stole quietly away in the darkness.

Studying the reports of the Battle of Monmouth, Frederick of Prussia exclaimed: "Clinton gained no advantage except to reach New York with his wreck of an army." The wreck might have been more complete if Lee had acted as ordered. He was arrested, tried by court-martial, and found guilty. In time he was dismissed from the army. Washington was not sorry to see him go.

243

TROUBLE BETWEEN FRIENDS

*The French fleet arrives,
bringing supplies and equipment,
but stays out of battle.*

On July 11, 1778, news of the arrival of a French fleet under Admiral d'Estaing stirred America. A swift move against the British fleet commanded by "Black Dick" Howe could leave Clinton's forces in New York at the mercy of Washington's army. Some Americans believed the end of the war was only weeks away. But d'Estaing was impressed by Howe's great reputation as a naval officer and refused to risk a battle.

Washington saw that there was another way to strike at the British. With the help of d'Estaing's ships and men, he could rid Rhode Island of the British army occupying Newport. But just as d'Estaing's fleet prepared for battle with the British ships protecting Newport, a storm separated the two fleets, and the action was never carried out.

The Americans settled down in New Jersey to camp through the fourth winter of the war. October brought supplies of coats, breeches, and shoes from France. The weather remained extremely mild and everyone was cheerful at Washington's headquarters at Middlebrook. "We danced all night," wrote General Henry Knox, describing one of the many social events that helped to while away the winter months. But elsewhere, in the Indian country, other Americans were passing the time in an entirely different manner.

Clark's rangers advanced despite the icy February floods.

War in the West

George Rogers Clark leads his rangers against the British and Indians.

The British, who held small forts along the Wabash and Mississippi Rivers, were playing a wicked game in the West. British commander Henry Hamilton had not won his nickname of "Hair Buyer" for nothing. Sending his agents among the Indians who lived north of the Ohio River, he had made clear that the hair he wished to buy was the scalps of American settlers. He told London that his aim was to stir up "alarm upon the frontiers of Virginia and Pennsylvania."

Down in the Kentucky country, young, red-headed George Rogers Clark had lived through many Indian raids, and had plans for an attack on the western outposts of the British and their Indian friends. Patrick Henry, who was now governor of Virginia, agreed with Clark. A small band of rangers was outfitted, and Clark plunged into the Illinois country. His rangers quickly captured the Indian settlements at Kaskaskia and Cahokia, but that was only half the job. The British still held Vincennes on the Wabash, and there would be no end to the Indian massacres until this post was taken.

Clark never lacked courage, and now he needed all he could muster. The weather in February, 1779, when Clark and his rangers started for Vincennes, was cold and raw. Eight days out of Kaskaskia the rangers reached the Little Wabash River, at a point where the river divides into two streams with about five miles of land between. Floodwater now covered every inch of that ground to a depth of three feet. Clark might have camped and waited—but he was not the kind of man who waits. He gave the order and his rangers plunged into the water.

George Rogers Clark

CLARK TAKES VINCENNES

It was a march none of them would ever forget. Water swirled around their hips at each stumbling step. The men groaned as the rifles they held aloft began to feel like the barrels of cannon. Their muscles tightened in agonizing knots. Those who became too sick to walk were towed along in canoes. At last they found a high spot of land where they could camp.

When the sun came up next day, George Rogers Clark suddenly sat upright. Had his ears tricked him? No, that was the sound of a gun. He was within "hearing distance" of the British garrison at Vincennes.

Later the rangers captured five Frenchmen in a canoe. The Frenchmen said that everyone in Vincennes knew that Clark and his boys were coming. The people were very

happy and the soldiers were very sad. But Clark could not reach Vincennes that night. The way ahead was too difficult, the floodwater too high.

But Clark intended to try, using his captured Frenchmen as guides. He scooped up a handful of water and mixed it with gunpowder. While the rangers watched, he blackened his face. Then, grinning, he gave a war whoop. They were going to Vincennes! One by one, they followed Clark.

Back in the water, they soon felt their feet grow numb in the slime. Shooting pains in their leg muscles made them cry aloud. Somehow they crawled along. They plunged into a flooded forest, where there were limbs to grasp and logs to keep the shorter men afloat. Finally, the water began to recede. Slowly they realized that they were making it. They were near Vincennes. With colors flying and drums beating, Clark and his boys marched toward town.

The battle that followed was fought viciously, but the rangers would not let anyone stop them after they had come so far. One of them described the fight as "fine sport for the Sons of Liberty." No one knew then how much they had won. But when the war ended, the conquest of Vincennes would give the United States a claim to lands as far west as the Mississippi and as far north as the Great Lakes.

THE WAR AT SEA

After raiding an English coastal town, John Paul Jones forces the British warship Serapis *to surrender following a hard battle.*

On the high seas, the war reached to distant places as the small American forces challenged the mighty British navy. From 1775 to 1783, British fighting ships increased from 270 to 468. Some 174 vessels carried sixty cannon or more. During the same period America succeeded in launching about one hundred armed cruisers and managed to sink or capture about 200 Brit-

ish ships. In addition, **American privateers** (armed ships, privately owned) **sank or captured 600 vessels.**

America's first naval hero was Jeremiah O'Brien, a New York lad who in 1775 lived in Machias, a town on the coast of Maine. O'Brien led an attack of sloops on the *Margaretta,* a British armed schooner **carrying** lumber to Gage's troops in Boston, **and** captured her. It was a hot one-hour battle sometimes called the "Lexington of the Sea."

Other naval heroes were David Bushnell, who built a one-man submarine, the *American Turtle,* and Esek Hopkins, who in 1775 commanded the little fleet that made up the first American navy.

But there was one man who stood out above the others—a Scottish sailor and one-

By capturing the Margaretta, *Jeremiah O'Brien became America's first naval hero.*

time slave trader whose real name was John Paul. When he joined the Americans as a privateer commander, he added Jones to his name, and let it be known that he preferred to be called Paul Jones.

In late April, 1778, Jones, commanding the *Ranger,* carried the war to Britain when he struck suddenly at Whitehaven on the northwest coast of England. About thirty armed Americans went ashore in two boats. They set fire to houses and ships in the harbor, and a London newspaper spoke of the scene as "too horrible" to describe.

Jones then staged a series of hit-and-run raids along the English coasts. At sunset on September 23, 1779, off Flamborough Head, he sighted a fleet of forty British merchantmen, escorted by the frigate *Serapis* and a smaller warship.

Aboard his flagship, the *Bon Homme Richard,* Jones turned to give battle to the *Serapis.* The *Bon Homme Richard* was severely battered by the foe. But when the British captain asked if the Americans were ready to surrender, Jones replied, "I have not yet begun to fight."

BATTLE AT SEA

Three hours later the greatest sea battle of the war ended with a victory for Jones. Lieutenant Richard Dale, who commanded a battery of twelve-pounders on the main deck of the *Bon Homme Richard,* wrote:

"The fire from the tops of the *Bon Homme Richard* was conducted with so much skill and effect as to destroy ulti-

The fight between the Serapis *and the* Bon Homme Richard *lasted late into the night.*

nately every man who appeared upon the quarter deck of the *Serapis,* and induced her commander to order the survivors to go below. Nor even under the shelter of the decks were they more secure. The powder-monkeys of the *Serapis,* finding no officers to receive the cartridges brought from the magazines, threw them on the main deck and went for more.

"These cartridges being scattered along the deck and numbers of them broken, it so happened that some of the hand-grenades thrown from the main-yard of the *Bon Homme Richard* . . . fell upon this powder and produced a most awful explosion. The effect was tremendous—more than twenty of the enemy were blown to pieces, and many stood with only the collars of their shirts upon their bodies. . . ."

Midshipman Nathaniel Fanning, who had been stationed as a lookout in the main-top of the *Bon Homme Richard,* described the closing moments of the American ship's victory:

"It was some time before the enemy's colors were struck. The captain of the *Serapis* gave repeated orders for one of his crew to ascend the quarter-deck and haul down the English flag, but no one would stir to do it. They told the captain they were afraid of our rifle-men. . . . The captain of the *Serapis* therefore ascended the quarter-deck, and hauled down the very flag which he had nailed to the flagstaff a little before the commencement of the battle, and which flag he had at that time, in the presence of his principal officers, swore he would never strike to that infamous pirate J. P. Jones."

Finally the British captain, who had sworn never to surrender to Jones, gave up.

At midnight, "Mad Anthony" Wayne and his men stormed the cliff to attack the British.

WASHINGTON AT A STANDSTILL

"Mad Anthony" Wayne takes Stony Point, but winter soon halts the fighting around New York.

The feats of George Rogers Clark in the Indian country and of John Paul Jones on the high seas did not solve Washington's problems in the spring of 1779. Fearing that the British would capture West Point and thus gain control of the highlands to the north, Washington scattered his forces to protect this fortress of the Hudson River.

Washington's idea was to sit tight and wait for Clinton to reveal his plans. Clinton, however, wanted to bring Washington out into the open for a full-scale battle, and the British raided King's Ferry on the Hudson and New Haven, Fairfield, Norwalk, and other Connecticut towns. The object was to tempt Washington to move from his protected position, but he refused to budge.

Meanwhile, British garrisons at Verplanck's Point and Stony Point guarded the two crossings at King's Ferry. In mid-July, after scouting the ground in person, Washington decided that a swift attack might recapture both points.

Veteran troops under Brigadier General "Mad Anthony" Wayne led the attack. The fort at Stony Point was set on a wooded cliff that stretched a half mile into the Hudson River and stood 150 feet above the water. Only a narrow strip of land over a marsh connected the fort with the mainland, and this became flooded at high tide. At midnight on July 16, 1779, with a bright moon shining, Wayne launched his attack.

Waiting inside their works at Stony Point, the redcoats yelled: "Come on, ye rebels! Come on!"

Wayne's boys called back: "Don't be in such a hurry, my lads. We will be with you presently."

The guns blazed and within twenty minutes Wayne had stormed his way almost to the fort. Falling with a scalp wound, Wayne cried: "Carry me up to the fort, boys. Let's go forward."

As Wayne's forces pounced upon the defenders of Stony Point, the redcoats—so said the New York *Journal*—raised a piteous shout: "Mercy! mercy! Dear Americans, mercy! Quarter! Brave Americans, quarter!" At any rate, the fort was quickly won.

Washington visited the fort two days later and ordered the works at Stony Point torn down. Wayne's boys carried off stores worth $158,640—prize money that they divided among themselves. As soon as the Americans left the dismantled fort, the British came back and rebuilt it. Sometimes the war seemed merely to go around in circles.

WINTER IN JOCKEY HOLLOW

A raid on Powle's Hook, a spit of sand opposite the lower end of Manhattan Island, ended Washington's campaign for 1779. Again the commander in chief withdrew his army for the winter, this time to settle near Morristown in a section of New Jersey known as Jockey Hollow.

In many ways the winter of 1779-80 was worse than the cruel months at Valley Forge. As badly clad as ever, the men struggled through enormous drifts as one howling snowstorm followed another. Even New Englanders could not remember a colder, more rugged winter than this one. For days the Hudson River was frozen solid across the 2,000 yards that separated New York from Powle's Hook.

Hunger haunted the soldiers in Jockey Hollow and one private declared that he saw several men "roast their old shoes and eat them." A mutinous uprising, though finally controlled, showed how close to the breaking point the men came.

251

TREASON AT WEST POINT

Benedict Arnold plots with the British to betray the Americans at West Point.

The British had a new plan for winning the war. It went into operation on December 29, 1778, when a strong British force landed two miles below the Savannah River in Georgia. By the end of February, 1779, the redcoats held Augusta and most of Georgia. Other British forces swept into South Carolina. While the British army in New York pinned down Washington, the redcoats were mopping up the southern colonies.

Washington could not afford to lose the South. Yet, if he went to the aid of the small American forces there, the British in New York might overrun his key defenses at West Point, which guarded the Hudson Valley.

Because West Point was so important, Washington had placed its defense in the hands of Benedict Arnold. Arnold had been angered when five junior officers were promoted ahead of him, but Washington thought highly of him. Arnold's new post was a big responsibility, for between New York and the Point there was nothing but a lawless neutral ground terrorized by two bands of armed outlaws. These were the "Cowboys," a gang of loyalist sympathizers, and the "Skinners," who called themselves "patriots."

In this region on a September day in 1780, a lone rider was suddenly stopped on the Tarrytown road by three men.

The rider gave his name as John Anderson and expressed the hope that the three men were Cowboy loyalists.

"We are," one said.

Anderson grinned. "So am I," he said. "I am a British officer on business of importance and must not be detained."

No sooner had he spoken than he realized that he had been trapped. The three men were Skinners. Anderson then said that he was really a patriot and, as proof, he produced a pass signed by General Benedict Arnold. The Skinners were not interested in the pass. They wanted money.

"Gentlemen, I have none about me," Anderson said.

"You said you were a British officer," the others said. All British officers had money. "Let's search him."

Benedict Arnold's treason was discovered when Major André, disguised and calling himself John Anderson, was captured by Skinners.

In Anderson's boot they found papers, but no money. Before the day ended those papers had been relayed to American officers, and had helped to uncover the ugliest story of the war.

John Anderson was, indeed, a British officer. His name, however, was Major John André. When the three Skinners caught him he was on his way to General Clinton with news that Arnold had agreed to betray West Point to the British. More than that, Arnold would tell Clinton where Washington would be staying on his way to Hartford, Connecticut—an open invitation to the enemy to capture the American commander in chief. For these services Arnold was to receive a British officer's commission and 20,000 pounds in cash.

This unhappy story of treachery went back to the time that the British held Philadelphia. Here André had been a friend of Peggy Shippen and had later come to know her husband, Arnold. When Arnold began to write letters to General Clinton offering to help the British for a price, Major André became the go-between.

Now André was tried by a jury of six generals. He had been captured in civilian dress, and so he was hanged as a spy.

Arnold escaped into Clinton's lines. He was made a British officer and received a traitor's fee, although it was not the 20,000 pounds he had been promised. Americans would despise him forever as the symbol of what General Nathanael Greene called "treason of the blackest dye."

LIVELY TIMES IN THE CAROLINAS

Charleston falls to the British, who fight savagely under "Bloody" Tarleton.

Meanwhile the war in the South boiled like a teakettle. A change came suddenly in early September of 1779, when the French fleet led by Admiral d'Estaing arrived at Savannah. D'Estaing's twenty-two French ships of the line and his eleven frigates were a powerful threat to the British, who had almost no naval support there. The troops of d'Estaing, added to American forces under General Benjamin Lincoln, gave the patriots an army of at least 5,000. The British in Savannah numbered about 3,200.

The French admiral demanded the surrender of Savannah, and the British stalled for time. They put slaves to work strengthening defenses, and reinforcements were rushed up from Port Royal. D'Estaing's guns lobbed shells into the town but did little damage to the British military installations. Rains in early October dampened everyone's spirits and d'Estaing decided that he would either storm Savannah or quit the place.

A heavy bombardment on October 9 opened the assault. French and American troops, becoming lost in a swamp, were mercilessly slaughtered. Still others, betrayed by a deserter, fell as they were led into a cross fire. A great friend of America, the Polish Count Casimir Pulaski, who had fought at Brandywine and Germantown, was mortally wounded by a cannon ball while leading a cavalry charge. The Americans lost more than 800 men, the British 150 at most.

D'Estaing, who had been severely wounded, sailed off with his ships and troops. The Americans raced back to Charleston to dig in for the bitter fight they could be sure was coming. Clinton sailed from New York with large British forces and three of his best officers—Earl Cornwallis, J. G. Simcoe, and Banastre Tarleton, who was known as "Bloody" Tarleton. In mid-February Clinton landed his troops on Jones Island, thirty miles from Charleston.

Within Charleston the patriots were in a tight spot. The forts that were intended to guard the city were in bad condition. Except for some cavalry left near Moncks Corner at the head of the Cooper River, General Lincoln drew his entire army in-

The Carolinas during the Revolution

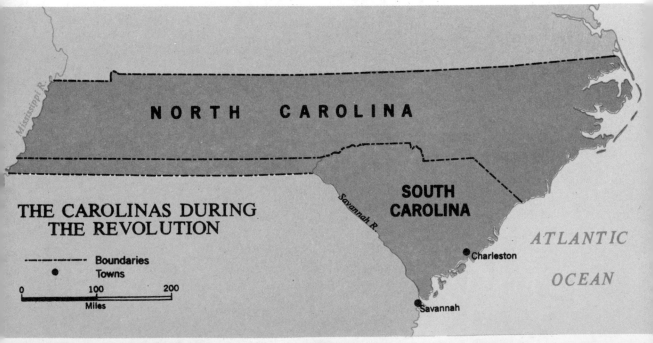

THE CAROLINAS DURING THE REVOLUTION

------- Boundaries
• Towns

0   100   200
Miles

The British opened up a heavy bombardment
on the entrenchments at Charleston.

Heavily outnumbered, the Americans were forced to retreat.

side Charleston. Since only a narrow isthmus, called the Neck, linked the city to the mainland, Lincoln had placed himself in a trap. His force at best numbered 5,000. Clinton had about 10,000 men.

When "Bloody" Tarleton struck savagely at Monck's Corner, routing Lincoln's cavalry, the jaws of the trap drew tighter. By the end of April the British had encircled Charleston so that there were no routes of escape. Three days later the siege rose to its greatest pitch, and General William Moultrie never forgot what he saw:

"The mortars from both sides threw out an immense number of shells. It was a glorious sight to see them like meteors crossing each other and bursting in the air. It appeared as if the stars were tumbling down. The fire was incessant almost the whole night, cannon balls whizzing and shells hissing constantly amongst us, ammunition chests and temporary magazines blowing up, great guns bursting, and wounded men groaning along the lines. It was a dreadful night! It was our last great effort, but it availed us nothing. After this, our military ardor was much abated. We began to cool, and we cooled gradually, and on the eleventh of May, we capitulated [surrendered]."

The militia and the armed civilians were free to go home, but Lincoln's soldiers laid down their arms as prisoners of war. During all the years of the Revolution, America would suffer no single loss to equal this.

And now Colonel Tarleton put in his licks. About 350 Virginia cavalrymen, under the command of Colonel Abraham Buford, were leading a supply train toward Salisbury when Tarleton caught up with them in the Waxhaws, a wooded region near the North Carolina border. "With the horrid yells of infuriated demons," Tarleton's men charged and General "Light-Horse Harry" Lee declared afterward, "This bloody day only wanted the war dance and the roasting fire to have placed it first in the records of torture and death in the West."

Buford, seeing he was clearly overwhelmed, raised a flag in surrender. But "Bloody" Tarleton showed no mercy, and wounded men were bayoneted in a scene of savage butchery.

CAMDEN AND KINGS MOUNTAIN

Southern patriots rally to wipe out a British force at a ridge known as Kings Mountain.

After the fall of Charleston, Clinton issued a harsh proclamation. The time had come, he said, when the people of the Carolinas must be either for or against the king. Those who helped the patriots would be hunted down and destroyed and their lands and homes seized. Anyone who aided in killing a loyalist would be treated as an enemy of the crown.

Meanwhile, with the capture of Benjamin Lincoln, Washington urged that the southern armies be placed under the command of that fiery Rhode Island Quaker, Nathanael Greene. But instead Congress chose Horatio Gates, the victor at Saratoga. General Gates prepared to attack the British at Camden, South Carolina, on the Wateree River, which the redcoats had occupied after the fall of Charleston.

Gates found his army on the verge of starvation, yet he ordered them to make ready to march. Of the two roads that led to Camden, Gates picked the one that offered the least chance to supply his forces. He fed his men on half-cooked meat, green corn, unripe peaches, and molasses. Suffering with weariness and bellyache, the Americans approached Camden.

Now Gates decided on a night march to surprise the Britishers. It happened that at the same time Cornwallis was marching his redcoats to surprise the Americans. The two armies, stumbling upon each other in the darkness, shared the surprise.

Francis Marion and his guerrillas kept raiding the British supply lines.

Climbing the craggy cliffs at Kings Mountain, the American forces defeated the British who had camped there for safety.

By daybreak, Cornwallis had his troops well placed for battle. Gates made the mistake of putting inexperienced militiamen in the center of his line. The fighting was desperate, but the Americans took a terrible drubbing and their losses that August 16, 1780, included about 1,000 casualties, 1,000 prisoners, and nearly all their guns. Gates jumped on a horse and joined his fleeing militia, covering sixty miles before he stopped. He rode himself out of the war.

The defeat and disorganization of the Americans at Camden endangered the patriot cause in the South. For a while, the only opposition to the British came from such daring guerrilla raiders as Francis Marion and Thomas Sumter. There were not enough of them to meet the enemy head on, but they struck hard and fast at British communications, cut up British detachments, and kept the southern loyalists from acting. Marion, a South Carolina planter and Indian fighter, was known as "the Swamp Fox." Whenever he was faced by too great a force, he faded into the marshlands where he could not be followed, then appeared at another point to bedevil the British again. Sumter, "the Gamecock," had served with Braddock in the French and Indian War and made the troops of "Bloody" Tarleton the special target of his raids.

Despite the raiders, however, Cornwallis advanced into North Carolina. He sent a force of about 1,000 soldiers under Major Patrick Ferguson to rally loyalist recruits in the western mountains. The patriots learned of this and came riding hard out of the north, south, east, and west.

Ferguson sought safety on a stony ridge between the two Carolinas known as Kings Mountain. He counted on the wooded and boulder-strewn slopes to protect him, but he was fighting woodsmen. These men could scamper nimbly over such ground, and they

259

could drop a squirrel with a single shot at fifty paces.

The Battle of Kings Mountain, fought October 7, 1780, was a stinging blow to British confidence. Among the Americans fighting that day was James P. Collins. The action was hot and it took three assaults for the Americans to gain the top of the cliff. "The enemy," Collins wrote, "was completely hemmed in on all sides, and no chance of escaping—besides, their leader [Major Ferguson] had fallen. After the fight was over . . . the dead lay in heaps on all sides, while the groans of the wounded were heard in every direction. I could not help turning away from the scene before me with horror and, though exulting in victory, could not refrain from shedding tears. . . ."

British losses that day were 400 casualties, 700 taken prisoner. The American losses totaled eighty-eight.

General Nathanael Greene

IN HANNAH'S COWPENS

Morgan prepares a "decent reception" for Tarleton's British army.

Congress now took Washington's advice and put Nathanael Greene in command of the southern army. Arriving at Charlotte, North Carolina, in December, Greene found his fighting force in need of guns, ammunition, wagons, food, and clothes. Opposing them were superior British troops, eager to pay back the Americans for the defeat on Kings Mountain.

During those early weeks, Greene's greatest ally in whipping the Americans into shape was Daniel Morgan, who had used a turkey call to rally his boys in the fighting at Saratoga. Morgan's test came on January 17, 1781, at a place called Hannah's Cowpens, thirty miles west of Kings Mountain.

The British were led by Colonel Tarleton, who was spoiling for revenge. Morgan, whose nickname was the "Old Wagoner," intended to give him a fight he would not forget. "Colonel Tarleton is said to be on his way to pay you a visit," Greene told Morgan. "I doubt not but he will have a decent reception. . . ."

The kind of "reception" that Morgan prepared for Tarleton at Cowpens was important, for it served as a model for a number of later battles fought in the South. Morgan planned his defense with the Broad River at his back, thus cutting off all possible retreat for his men.

Morgan was supremely confident, telling his troops the night before that "as sure as he lived, the Old Wagoner would crack his whip" over Tarleton in the morning. He placed his army in three lines—his raw militia in front, then his seasoned Continentals, and his cavalry in the rear. Each line was to fire two volleys at the British before falling back to the next line of defense.

Lured into Morgan's trap at Cowpens, the British turned and ran for their lives.

As Tarleton approached Cowpens, it seemed to him that Morgan was the silliest of fools. Why, a frontal bayonet attack would send those raw militiamen scurrying for their lives! And Morgan's men did indeed begin to fall back under the first British charge. Tarleton believed he had his battle won. He threw in his reserves, and the British charged in wild disorder. But Morgan, knowing exactly what he was about, threw his cavalry across Tarleton's line of retreat. Thomas Young, fighting with the Americans that morning, reported: "The British broke, and throwing down their guns and cartouche [ammunition] boxes, made for the wagon road and did the prettiest sort of running!"

That day 110 Britishers were killed and 702 were taken prisoner. The booty the Americans collected included 800 muskets, one hundred horses, thirty-five wagons of baggage, and sixty Negro slaves. Morgan's loss was twelve killed, sixty wounded.

Tarleton's disaster at Cowpens, said Earl Cornwallis, "almost broke my heart." One third of his British army had been swept away. Meanwhile, Greene was playing his own game, luring Cornwallis northward.

Cornwallis chased Greene grimly, meeting him in battle at Guilford Court House, North Carolina, on March 15, 1781. Although Greene tried to do the same kind of fighting that Morgan had done at Cowpens, he failed to make effective use of his cavalry. 261

As a result, when the day ended, Cornwallis held the field and had captured Greene's guns. Yet British losses had been heavy—about one fourth of the force—so that in London a critic said: "Another such victory will destroy the British army!"

Cornwallis was in a peculiar situation. Greene now had lured him 200 miles from his main base, and Marion's and Sumter's forces were raising hob with attacks on British outposts. Cornwallis appealed to Clinton in New York, begging him to bring all British forces into Virginia.

Meanwhile, Cornwallis had to get back to the sea. If he returned to Camden, he would apparently be admitting defeat. He decided, therefore, to march his army down the Cape Fear River to the port of Wil-

mington, North Carolina, and from Wilmington into Virginia.

But Greene decided to march south and try to win back South Carolina and Georgia. The British left behind at Camden beat him repeatedly in a series of small battles, but their victories gained nothing.

WASHINGTON AND ROCHAMBEAU

A French army under Rochambeau and a fleet under de Grasse join Washington.

In May of 1781, Washington left his headquarters at West Point to meet in the

Americans welcomed French General Rochambeau and his trim, well-disciplined troops.

and was now a brigadier general in the British army. Arnold took Richmond, made a number of raids, and then withdrew to Portsmouth. Cornwallis also reached Virginia, and the British were threatening to take control of the state. Meanwhile, Lafayette was moving south at the head of 1,200 American troops.

Washington believed Clinton's position was weak, and he asked Rochambeau to join him in an attack on New York City. Rochambeau felt it might be better to strike at the British in Virginia, but he agreed to do as Washington asked. In either case, the Americans needed the support of the French fleet, which was now in the West Indies. Washington and Rochambeau sent messages to the commander of the fleet, Admiral François de Grasse. They left it up to him to decide whether to sail to New York or Virginia.

In July Rochambeau's troops joined Washington's at Dobbs Ferry, New York, but by August several important things had happened in the South. Arnold had been replaced by another general, and his force combined with that of Cornwallis. More reinforcements arrived, giving Cornwallis about 7,500 men. Lafayette had only about 3,000 men, even after he had been joined by Anthony Wayne and von Steuben. He wisely refused to let the British get him into a big battle. He fought small skirmishes, each time slipping away from the enemy.

Cornwallis was also having trouble with Clinton, who remained in New York. Clinton's orders changed from one day to the next. At first he wanted 3,000 troops sent back to New York; then he did not want them; then he wanted them again. At last he told Cornwallis to keep the troops and allowed him to go to Yorktown, off the entrance to Chesapeake Bay.

Washington and Rochambeau were mak-

pleasant little village of Wethersfield, Connecticut, with a most remarkable Frenchman. The previous summer, Count Jean de Rochambeau had reached Newport, Rhode Island, with 5,000 French troops. Now fifty-five years of age, an experienced military leader, and a gentleman of great charm and tact, Rochambeau had quickly won the hearts of the New Englanders. His troops were extremely well behaved, paid in gold for what they used, and dazzled the ladies with their colorful uniforms.

As Washington journeyed to Wethersfield, he had two problems on his mind—New York and Virginia. Clinton still held New York City, and that winter he had sent a force into Virginia. It was led by Benedict Arnold, the traitor who had changed sides

General Charles Cornwallis

ing preparations to attack New York when, on August 14, news came from Admiral de Grasse. He was sailing to Chesapeake Bay with twenty-eight warships and several transports carrying 3,000 French troops. Washington immediately decided to attack the British in Virginia. He would swing around New York, hiding his intentions from Clinton, and then race to Virginia to catch Cornwallis in Yorktown. With the French fleet blockading Chesapeake Bay—the only route by which the British could escape or receive reinforcements—Washington would have Cornwallis neatly trapped.

264

WASHINGTON OUTWITS CLINTON

Pretending to threaten New York, Washington moves his army to Virginia to trap Cornwallis.

On August 19, Washington began to move his army from Dobbs Ferry. Clinton believed that the American commander was playing the same old game of coming across

New Jersey for an attack on New York. Washington was careful to keep his plans secret so that no spy or deserter could reveal them to Clinton.

American and French forces moved through New Jersey in three columns. One wing of the army went through Morristown, Somerset Court House, and Princeton; a second through Bound Brook and Somerset; a third through New Brunswick and Trenton. To make it look as though he were going to attack New York, Washington set up French ovens and warehouses at Chatham. He then pushed his forces ahead, knowing that if his columns could meet at Princeton and Trenton before Clinton awoke to his objective, the race to Virginia was practically won.

The plan worked perfectly. On the last two days of August, the American troops passed through Princeton to Trenton. Washington and Rochambeau, ahead of the armies, were already receiving a hero's welcome in Philadelphia. The Continentals paraded through the streets of the Quaker City on September 2, with drums beating

and fifes playing. Next day Rochambeau led his smartly uniformed soldiers through the city.

Clouds of dust, wrote an eyewitness, fell "like a smothering snow-storm." But cheering Philadelphians forgot this nuisance as they shouted and sang. Steadily the Americans and French pressed on to Virginia, and one observer remarked: "General Washington and the army are gone to take Lord Cornwallis in his mousetrap."

Like the pieces in a puzzle, other events fell into place. By the end of August, the French fleet under de Grasse was anchored in Lynnhaven Bay off Hampton Roads. Meanwhile, Lafayette moved quickly to throw a strong defensive line across the peninsula at Williamsburg so that Cornwallis would be tightly sealed into his Yorktown "mousetrap." Early September brought a battle off the Virginia coast between the French fleet and the British under Rear Admiral Thomas Graves. The Britishers, discouraged if not beaten, limped back to New York.

September 9 was a great day for Wash-

Washington's routes through New Jersey

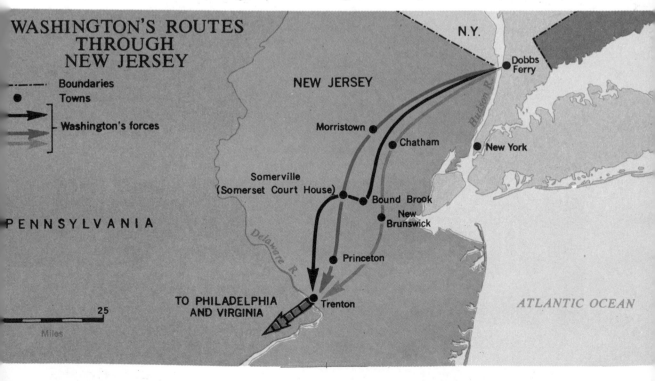

ington. For the first time since May 4, 1775, he visited his home in Mount Vernon. By mid-September, he reached Williamsburg.

"Men, women and children," wrote Colonel St. George Tucker, who was in command of the militia, "seemed to vie with each other in demonstrations of joy and eagerness to see their beloved countryman." Lafayette rushed forward, "clasped the general in his arms, and embraced him with an ardor not easily described."

Cannon boomed in welcome and Colonel Tucker wrote in his diary: "Cornwallis may now tremble for his fate, for nothing but some extraordinary intervention of his guardian angels seems capable of saving him and the whole army from captivity."

Victory AT YORKTOWN

Trapped and outnumbered, the British and Hessians fight bravely, but Cornwallis is forced to surrender.

On September 28, Washington moved on Yorktown. Cornwallis tried to put up a brave front, but hastily withdrew into his inner lines of defense, and Washington's troops quickly occupied his "outer works."

Mount Vernon

Washington turned to the hard work of building entrenchments and moving up his heavy guns. Joseph Plumb Martin, who had been fighting with the Continentals since the retreat from Long Island in 1776, was amused as he watched Washington strike "a few blows with a pickaxe, a mere ceremony, that it might be said, 'General Washington with his own hands first broke ground at the siege of Yorktown.'"

YORKTOWN BOMBARDED

By October 9, Washington had his big guns in place, and the bombardment of Yorktown began. Quickly the city became a deathtrap. Citizens and soldiers alike rushed to hide against the sand banks of the York River, and there was a report that even Cornwallis was living underground. The diary of a Hessian soldier described the deadliness of Washington's guns:

"During these 24 hours 3,600 shots were counted from the enemy, which they fired at the town, our line, and at the ships in the harbor. These ships were miserably ruined and shot to pieces. Also the bombs and cannon balls hit many inhabitants and Negroes of the city, and marines, sailors, and soldiers. One saw men lying nearly everywhere who were mortally wounded and whose heads, arms, and legs had been shot off. . . ."

Washington's forces, outnumbering those of Cornwallis 16,000 to 7,500, were spread in a semicircle around his foe. As his army dug its trenches ever closer to the enemy, the key to winning Yorktown became two British outposts—Redoubts Nine and Ten.

On October 14, a Sunday night, dark with "a thick fog," a Hessian sentry on Redoubt Ten, hearing a movement, cried out, *"Wer da?"*—"Who's there?" He soon found that it was a French force carrying "long storming spikes." At Redoubt Nine, American troops under Colonel Alexander Hamilton also charged out of the misty night to surprise the enemy.

Alexander Hamilton led his troops in the charge on Redoubt Nine.

The fog turned to rain. Shouts, curses, groans filled the night. "As I mounted the breastwork," wrote young Martin, "I met an old associate hitching himself down into the trench. I knew him by the light of the enemy's musketry, it was so vivid." A cry rang out from the French, *"Vive le Roi!"* —"Long live the king!" They had won Redoubt Ten. Soon the Americans were bayoneting their way into the other fort.

THE BRITISH GIVE IN

The end was near for Cornwallis. Sixteen large boats were assembled to ferry his forces across the York River to Gloucester, but a violent windstorm swept his boats down-river. Washington's big guns continued pounding the town until a Hessian, viewing a scene "even more horrible than ever before . . . saw nothing but bombs and balls raining on our whole line."

At ten o'clock on the morning of October 16, 1781, a drummer mounted a British parapet. He beat a parley calling for talks between the two opposing leaders. A British officer appeared outside the fort. He waved a white handkerchief. The American guns fell silent. Except for arranging the terms of the surrender, the Battle of Yorktown had ended.

At two o'clock on the afternoon of October 19, Washington rode on his white horse to receive the formal surrender of Cornwallis' army. With him were the beaming Rochambeau, the smiling Lafayette. The sun shone brightly. A Virginia militiaman, gazing at the handsomely dressed French soldiers, realized that they were not, as he once believed, a people who lived "on frogs and coarse vegetables."

As the redcoats came down the road to the doleful piping of their fifes, one American believed that "the British officers in general behaved like boys who had been whipped at school. Some bit their lips, some pouted, some cried." Cornwallis refused to attend the humiliating scene.

The British and Hessians heard the command, "Ground arms and take off cartridge boxes and sabers." Solemnly they obeyed.

On the afternoon of October 19, 1781, the British surrendered. Major General Benjamin Lincoln accepted the sword from British General O'Hara while Washington looked on.

"OUR BELOVED GENERAL WAVED HIS HAT"

The war over, Washington bids good-by to his officers and returns to Mount Vernon.

Washington's "Victory Dispatch" from Yorktown did not reach the Continental Congress until October 24. An old German watchman awakened Philadelphians that morning with the joyous shout: *"Basht dree o'glock, und Cornval-lis isht daken!"* News of the British surrender, traveling through the colonies, produced celebrations everywhere. At Newburgh, New York, the people "hanged and burnt in effigy the traitor Arnold." When information of the disaster was received in London, Lord North, pacing the floor, cried out: "Oh God! It is all over!"

But wars do not end easily. George III seemed as determined as ever to carry on the conflict. Washington was afraid that Americans would grow careless, let down their guard, and lose everything they had gained.

Months went by. The government in England changed, bringing into power persons who favored granting independence to America. Then it changed back and the "war party" once more gained control.

Sir Henry Clinton was removed as commander of British troops in New York. His successor, Sir Guy Carleton, was a genial Irishman who hinted broadly that peace was near.

A year went by. Soldiers quarreled over their idleness, poor provisions, and lack of pay. A cold, bitter winter added to the misery.

Then on April 19, 1783—exactly eight years to the day after the redcoats had fired at the Minutemen on Lexington Green—the army received an announcement. There

As the barge that was to carry him home moved into the river, the general turned and waved his hat in farewell.

was to be an official "cessation of hostilities between the United States of America and the King of Great Britain."

On November 25, 1783, with the British gone at last from New York, Washington rode into the city. A dinner in his honor was followed by a "splendid display of fireworks" on lower Broadway. Now free to return home to his beloved Mount Vernon, Washington bade farewell to his officers.

"I cannot come to each of you," he said, "but shall feel obliged if each of you will come and take me by the hand."

General Henry Knox, the Boston bookseller who had fought for freedom since the days of Breed's Hill, embraced his commander in chief with tears streaming down his cheeks. The others came up, each in turn showing his deep affection. The feelings of the occasion were well understood by Lieutenant Colonel Benjamin Tallmadge:

"The simple thought that we were then about to part from the man who had conducted us through a long and bloody war, and under whose conduct the glory and the independence of our country had been achieved, and that we should see his face no more in this world, seemed to me utterly insupportable.

"But the time of separation had come, and waving his hand to his grieving children around him, and passing through a corps of light infantry who were paraded to receive him, he walked silently on to Whitehall, where a barge was in waiting. We all followed in mournful silence to the wharf, where a prodigious crowd had assembled to witness the departure of the man who, under God, had been the great agent in establishing the glory and independence of these United States. As soon as he was seated, the barge put off into the river, and when out in the stream, our great and beloved General waved his hat and bid us a silent adieu."

Home, Washington thought—he was going home at last, to live out his years in peace at Mount Vernon. But only the opportunity to be free had been won—a nation still remained to be built. And so a day would come when Washington would return to this city, stand before other cheering crowds, and, raising his hand, take the oath of office as the first President of the United States.

271

BUILDING THE NATION

*Once the Revolution had been won, Americans found
themselves faced with the problem of setting
up their own government. Volume IV, Building the Nation,
describes their struggles and difficulties,
and tells how a group of men met in Philadelphia
and wrote the Constitution.
The Constitution did not, of course, solve all
the problems facing the new nation,
but it did provide a framework under which free men
could govern themselves.
As the years went on, America fought another war
with England, expanded its borders westward,
and saw the beginning of a national disagreement over the
slavery question which, in time, would split the
new nation in two. Yet in spite of everything,
America prospered and grew strong.
Building the Nation covers the years 1783-1850.*

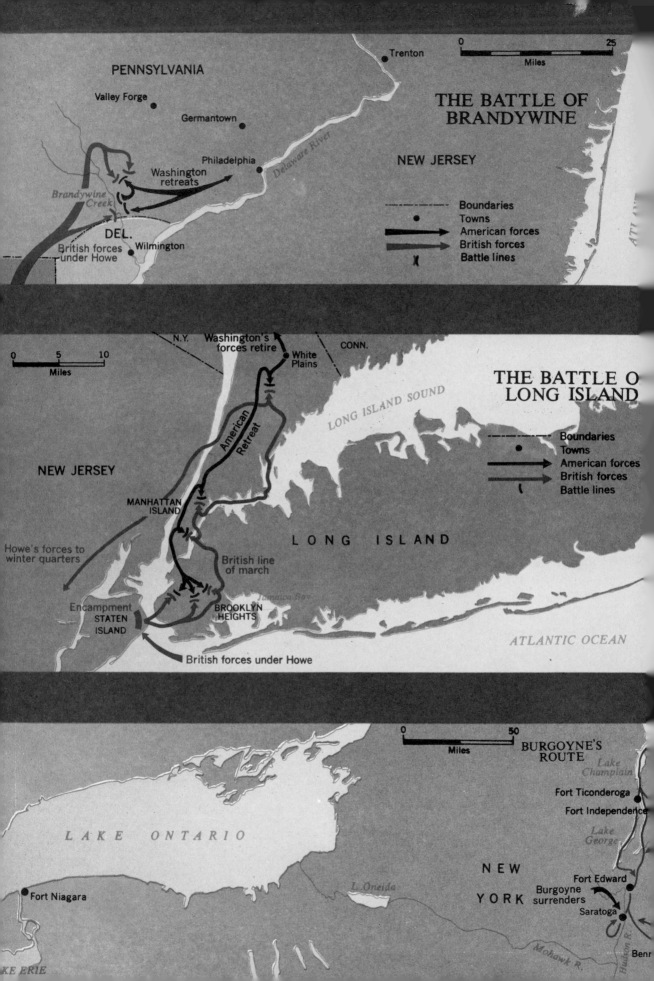

THE BATTLE OF BRANDYWINE

PENNSYLVANIA

Valley Forge

Germantown

Trenton

NEW JERSEY

Philadelphia

Washington retreats

Delaware River

Brandywine Creek

DEL.

Wilmington

British forces under Howe

0   25
Miles

Boundaries
Towns
American forces
British forces
Battle lines

THE BATTLE O LONG ISLAND

N.Y.   Washington's forces retire

CONN.

White Plains

LONG ISLAND SOUND

American Retreat

NEW JERSEY

MANHATTAN ISLAND

LONG ISLAND

Howe's forces to winter quarters

British line of march

Jamaica Bay

Encampment STATEN ISLAND

BROOKLYN HEIGHTS

ATLANTIC OCEAN

British forces under Howe

0   5   10
Miles

Boundaries
Towns
American forces
British forces
Battle lines

BURGOYNE'S ROUTE

0   50
Miles

Lake Champlain

Fort Ticonderoga

Fort Independence

Lake George

LAKE ONTARIO

NEW YORK

Fort Edward

Burgoyne surrenders

Fort Niagara

L. Oneida

Saratoga

Mohawk R.

Benn

Hudson R.

KE ERIE